SEVEN STEPS

to

EVERYDAY MYSTICISM

SEVEN STEPS

to

EVERYDAY MYSTICISM

Patsy Scala

Ivy House
Publishing Group
www.ivyhousebooks.com

11/04

PUBLISHED BY IVY HOUSE PUBLISHING GROUP
5122 Bur Oak Circle, Raleigh, NC 27612
United States of America
919-782-0281

ISBN: 1-57197-326-5
Library of Congress Control Number: 2002101712

Printed in the United States of America

L

DEDICATION

To my mother, Patricia O'Rourke Money, for her love, for her poetry, and for her mysticism;

To my father, John David Money, for his love, and for his belief that I could achieve my wildest dreams;

To my daughter, Laura Scala, for *being* love, for being my greatest teacher, and for being my closest friend;

To my husband, Joseph Scala, for his enduring love and his sense of humor;

To my former son-in-law, and forever friend, Ken Souser, for his support and for his intelligence and discernment;

To my in-laws: my father-in-law, Joseph Scala, Sr., for his ability to embrace the joy in every day; my mother-in-law, Lillian Carlo Scala, for accepting me as a daughter rather than a daughter-in-law; and Aunt Elsie Carlo, for showing me that age is a delight, not a limitation;

To my spiritual teachers, especially Daniel and Love Douglas and Shay St. John, for their guidance and prayers;

To the family of my godchild, Glenna Price: Win, Eileen, Islen, Glenna, and Gaelyn, for teaching me to "Say YES to life!"

To my dear friends, for their support and love (in alphabetic order), Maureen and Rob Bishop, Stewart Brisby, Sheri and Rod Buchen, Joy Fragola, Paul Horton, Michael Ristau, and Carol and David Upright;

To my dogs Buggsey and Tippy, and my "granddog" Bailey, for teaching me every day the true meaning of unconditional love;

To the Neville Brothers for the spiritual message in their music;

And especially to God, who is in all . . . and in all is all love.

THE ESSENCE OF MYSTERY

When you pluck the petals from the rose,
The flower is no more—
'Twas the wholeness of it,
The beauty and the fragrance of it,
The eternal mystery of it,
That was the allure.

—Patricia O'Rourke Money

INTRODUCTION

What *is* mysticism?

How does it help in our daily lives?

And isn't it boring?

What is mysticism? . . . And, beyond that, why would we want to experience it in our everyday lives? . . . Is it really possible to make the Universe work for us and with us? . . . And, for heaven's sake (literally) why would we want to find God wherever we look? . . in an ice cream cone, for example . . . or in a traffic jam . . . or at our desks at work?

Walter Starcke, in his metaphysical book *It's All God*, defines mysticism in this way:

> Mysticism is the belief that direct knowledge of God, of spiritual truth, of ultimate reality is attainable through intuition, insight, or illumination in a way differing from ordinary sense perception. Anyone who has the capacity to listen to his or her inner voice and speak from Spirit is a mystic. All true mystics have had the same experience—a peek into an underlying reality where their individual self has merged with infinite beingness, an experience that is really beyond words and thoughts. Each has seen, or for a moment has become, the light.

There are many definitions of mysticism, but there is typically one predominant *picture* of the mystic: He is ascetic, thin, serious, probably dour, seated atop a Tibetan mountain, legs in classic lotus position, eyes downcast. This would be a difficult image to live up to in everyday life. More to the point, why would we *want* to?

My definition of mysticism is more general: A mystic is a person who, for the most part (although not always . . . we are human, after all) approaches the recognition of his or her oneness with all things. The mystic feels unity with the crow sitting on the topmost branch of a tree . . . the mystic senses the energy of the wind, the rain, a waterfall . . . The mystic *knows* that there is one energy pervading and creating all things, and that this energy is often called God. The mystic has experienced this energy. The mystic is very much like me. The mystic is probably embodied in you, as well.

At the most perfect moments, the mystic looks *from* the eyes of God *into* the eyes of God, no matter what she or he is seeing. Because of this recognition of oneness, the mystic is at peace with whatever happens. The mystic feels love for all things, and joy comes easily, through simple things.

The everyday mystic may choose at times to sit cross-legged on a mountaintop. More often, we will find her in a business suit at a conference table; we will see him in spandex and running shoes on a treadmill.

Mystics look like ordinary people.

But unlike ordinary people, they are able to use *all* the resources of the Universe to accomplish their goals. They know how to manifest good.

Life is easier for the mystic.

Mystics are like the butterfly, which, by fluttering its wings in China, changes rainfall patterns in the Congo. Instantly.

In addition, the mystic tends to find the sacred in all things, not just those things that are deemed holy by churches. And what is sacred? It is anything which we honor simply because it is true to what it is created to be. A forest is sacred space, as it follows perfectly the cycles of nature's seasons. A hawk is sacred as it soars through the sky. Our food, and those people who process and prepare it, are sacred as they serve the nutritional needs of the planet.

And we too, all of us, are sacred . . . at least in the deepest, purest part of ourselves. The mystic knows this, and honors this sacredness in all that is . . . and in every other human.

The mystic also knows that he or she is united . . . truly one . . . with all other people and things. S/he knows this on a deep and personal level . . . *feels* the closeness that comes from knowing that the very air we breathe in was given to us from the trees we stand under and the grass we walk on. And that, when we breathe out, we nourish these same plants. And s/he knows that the molecules that nourish us could, at some time, have been molecules in the bodies of Jesus, or Buddha, or the drunk who panhandled us yesterday.

Physicists tell us that energy can be neither created nor destroyed. Mystics *know* this . . . *sense* it. And know that this energy which unites us all can be called God.

Mystics can indeed find God in an ice cream cone . . . and in everything else that exists.

To be mystics, we don't have to be saints. Mysticism isn't a boring path of seriousness. Rather it can be great fun . . . as well as spiritually fulfilling . . . to live life as an everyday mystic. The mystic knows how to live peacefully "in the flow." The mystic knows how to use synchronicity to manifest goodness (and the proverbial good parking spaces).

The mystic knows how to create grand results with little effort.

The mystic, in short, knows how to live life fully, as a complete and joyful human being.

Each of us recognizes the mystic in us in different ways. I don't know at what precise moment you will know that you have become an everyday mystic. I can, however, share my story with you.

I always knew that my mother was different from other children's mothers.

For starters, she paid little if any attention to things that a proper housewife was supposed to do. She prepared meals only because it was necessary that we eat. She cleaned the house only when I had begun to name the dust balls. Although she was a stunningly beautiful woman, she cared little for fashion and not at all for makeup.

But oh . . . she could speak eloquently about the song of a bird. The crimsons and golds of autumn leaves filled her with joy. And she wrote poetry . . . beautiful treatises on the things she loved, from the birth of Christ . . . to the art within a slab of marble . . . to a tree in springtime.

These things were all sacred to my mother. She saw the presence of God in all of it.

I remember going for a walk with her one evening. The sky was deep blue, with stars so numerous that it looked as if someone had flung diamonds across the dark expanse.

She stopped in the middle of the road and exclaimed, "How is it possible to look at a sky like this and not see God?" her voice filled with joy and awe. I, then about 13, was looking at the sky thinking about the romantic possibilities with one or another of my boyfriends under a star-studded sky.

My mother, I thought, saw things differently from the way I saw them.

But, then again, her childhood had been vastly different from mine. She had been orphaned as a tiny child, and placed into a series of foster homes. When she was barely six years old, she was living with a family who insisted that she scrub their floors, do their washing (by hand and washboard, of course), and clean their dishes. In return, they beat her.

When she had been with this family for almost a year, an epidemic of tuberculosis broke out, killing every member of the family. My mother remained in perfect health, and was discovered by a Catholic priest named Father Cavanaugh, who was the director of a boarding school for girls, St. Claire Academy, in a small Wisconsin town. The school "adopted" my mother and gave her a home.

There she roamed the wooded acres, wrote poetry under massive trees, studied literature, the arts, theology, philosophy. There she became a mystic.

My childhood was filled with playmates, fights with the boy across the street, piano lessons, and much normalcy, crowned with an overwhelming swell of love from my mother and my father.

It was natural that I didn't see things quite the way my mother did. She had experienced pain and separation. She had also experienced spirituality as a daily discipline, living as she did with nuns and priests. She had experienced extremes; my early experiences were ordinary.

Or so it seemed to me, as I was living them. In retrospect, my early life had some real uniqueness.

My father was a draft resister and a pacifist, not a popular belief system . . . especially for someone who was also a successful businessman. Sometimes I would awake to find strangers sleeping on the couch and the floor in our living room.

"They are friends," my mother would explain. They were also draft resisters, hiding out, for a while, in our home.

I remember one night, sitting in the living room with these adults, as they discussed the then current war. At the time, I was three or four years old, and very bored with their discussion.

"Can we stop talking about this?" I asked. "The war is going to end next Tuesday," I added with certainty. And I did feel certain about it, although I don't know how.

Rather than trivialize my comment, my parents thanked me for my input. And when the war did, in fact, end the next Tuesday, they praised my wisdom to all their friends. They thought it was wonderful that I had known.

I didn't think much about it at all.

As I was growing up, my father sometimes took me to the Methodist church where his brother-in-law was the preacher. More often, he went fishing, where he could be in touch with nature . . . where he could experience the presence of his version of God.

When we went to the little church across the street from where he grew up, however, I was enchanted by the rich, rolling baritone voice of my uncle, as he talked about living a Christian life. I paid little attention to his content, but his passion never failed to move me.

More often, I went to a Catholic church with my mother. This church was as large as my father's was small . . . a massive stone structure on top of a hill in the middle of the city. Its marble vestibule was imposing, almost frightening. Inside, there was the smell of incense, the chanting of the choir, and the priest intoning what I guessed were prayers in a language I didn't understand. If I rarely listened to what my uncle said in his sermons, I couldn't comprehend what was said in my mother's church, even if I had listened.

The church was filled with something palpable, though . . . something that was deeply appealing to me. I would try to let go of my thoughts and just absorb the ancient music, the foreign words, the rich and exotic aromas. I tried just to experience the feeling of this building in which, for many years, prayers and supplications had risen to a God that was somewhere, in a place called heaven.

To me, it felt as if there was a powerful energy right there in that massive stone church . . . the same kind of energy that filled my father's tiny church when my uncle's deep voice rose in prayer.

I tried, and often succeeded, in losing my conscious self to these sounds and aromas . . . to the *energy* in the very different churches. If someone had suggested that I was meditating, I wouldn't have known what he or she was talking about. If anyone had said that I was having a mystical experience, I would have denied it utterly. Cute little girls in the South didn't have mystical experiences.

When I was eleven years old, I had one of those experiences that we now call "watershed experiences." Something that would forever change my life and alter my perceptions of who I was and what life was about. My father's health began to falter. His speech began to fail. He was diagnosed with a malignant brain tumor. In early December, he died.

The night he died, my mother and I were having dinner at our home. She appeared startled for an instant, then told me that we needed to leave our food and go immediately to the hospital. I was used to the fact that my mother *knew* things, so I went without question. She, of course, had experienced the exact moment of my father's death.

Later that night, as her friends gathered around her in support, I lay alone in my bedroom. My mother and her friends were not ignoring me. They thought I was asleep. Instead, I was feeling the most utter loneliness and sadness that I have ever felt. If I had known the meaning of the word "bereft" I might have described the way I felt in that way.

Suddenly, there was a brilliant, sparkling and pulsating light at the foot of my bed. My father, now healthy again, stood in the midst of the light, his body real, yet evanescent.

He smiled at me and said, "I am all right. I am at peace. I love you." The light grew brighter, and I could hear the tinkling of thousands of tiny bells. And my father and the light disappeared as quickly as they had appeared. I slept, at peace . . . knowing without any doubt that I had indeed seen my father.

Again, if someone had told me that I had had a mystical experience, I would have dismissed the very thought of it.

When I told my mother what had happened, fully expecting her to explain to me why I couldn't possibly have seen my father, she smiled and leaned back on the couch.

"Yes," she said. "That is very possible. When I was a little girl living with a foster family, the family all came down with a serious disease. I was afraid, and one night, at the foot of my bed, I saw a boy child, surrounded in light. It was the most beautiful thing I have ever seen. He told me that I was going to be all right. Later, when I saw pictures of the Christ Child in books, I realized that it was Christ who had come to me."

I believed her utterly . . . believed because it seemed natural that something magical would happen to her . . . believed because I had seen so many other manifestations of her understanding of the mysterious.

If I had known the meaning of "mystic," I would have accepted without question her mysticism. I also would have, without question, denied my own.

And, even if I had put my adult understanding and wisdom to the question of whether or not I was a mystic, I would have looked at this young girl growing up in Tennessee and said, "No, it's not likely. There's nothing in her life that suggests even a tiny modicum of mysticism."

And history would have supported me.

My mother, having been reared in a Catholic convent, spent her formative years literally breathing in the mysterious and wonderful rituals of Catholicism every day. The incense was her perfume; the nuns her friends. The most common music of her days was the chant.

And she was fully Irish . . . 100% . . . and the Irish are known for their belief in the mystic, the magical, the ability to "know" without any means of knowing.

Of course, I, too was mostly Irish, but I didn't think of it that way. My father's family was part French, and my youthful conceits grabbed onto everything French. If the Irish have their leprechauns and spirits, the French have fashion and makeup and elegance. I dove into clothes and makeup as passionately as my mother ignored it.

Still . . . odd things happened to me. Up until the time of my father's death, my eyes had been blue, like his. My mother, on the other hand, had bottle green eyes. After his death, my eyes became blue-green. It was as if a physical part of both my parents had created some mid-youth change in me. I thought it was weird, but the result was not awe, but a rush to buy new makeup colors. (After my mother died, my eyes turned green, and by that time, I was old enough to feel the awe . . . to recognize the mystery. But I'm jumping ahead.)

As I entered my teens, I loved to go into a Catholic church to hear mass very early on weekday mornings. Again, I paid no attention at all to what was going on liturgically, but I reveled in the feeling of it . . . in its strange energy. It was almost possible for me to believe that this place was, indeed, the house of God, although I really didn't understand who God was. When I went to mass on Sundays, I was too interested in the boys in attendance to feel any spiritual energy . . . and the church was always too packed. The early weekday masses often had me as a lone worshiper.

Not that I was particularly religious. In fact, as I grew older . . . even though I attended a Catholic college for my undergraduate work . . . I became more and more skeptical about the existence of the Divine. I just couldn't comprehend how there could be a man in the sky somewhere who knew all about everything I did with boys . . . or, more to the point, who would *care*.

The poetry of the Beats was more intriguing. Sometimes, when I was listening to poetry, I almost felt that wonderful, ecstatic energy that I felt in empty churches. I never associated it with God. So I dressed in black turtlenecks and jeans and contemplated the meaning of my existence.

And sometimes, I would join my mother in her delight over the first touch of warmth on an early spring day . . . or the first reds of autumn. We would talk, and sometimes I would think I was just about to "get it," whatever "it" was. I would feel as if I was on the edge of something. And then I'd be back to worrying about how I should fix my hair for the next party.

It must say something about me . . . and is most assuredly a tribute to my mother's creativity . . . that I finally married an artist. I also began to write, never associating my own writing with what my mother did. I noticed that, when I wrote, I was often not conscious of what was going down on paper. It was as if my words were being written *for* me. I never placed any mystical meaning on this, either.

After I married, I gave up the Church. Actually, two things drove me away. The first, as it was for so many young women, was the Church's stand on birth control. The second was my last time as a serious participant in a Catholic mass.

My husband and I were in a church, listening to the pre-sermon announcements, and the priest announced a workshop: "Celibacy as a Cure for Loneliness" . . . for married couples only. The irony . . . and the cruelty . . . and the interference of organized religion in human lives . . . was staggering.

I turned to my husband, said, "I'm out of here," and left.

At this point in my life, I was entering a period of life-building, and I had little time, and even less desire, to explore spirituality. I associated all that was spiritual with the Church, and I was angry with the Church. Even after the anger slipped away, there was complete disinterest in anything canonical.

My husband and I had a child, a beautiful dark-eyed daughter, whom we named Laura, and all my psychic energy was sent to her. It never occurred to me that the tremendous love that I felt for her . . . or the oneness I experienced when I breast-fed her very early in the morning as the sun rose . . . had anything to do with spirituality. It was simply, and only, the love of a mother for her child.

My mother watched Laura when I went back to work and, as she always had, she related the wonder of childbirth to the wonder of God. She saw the union . . . the oneness. She felt the awe. Caring for Laura seemed to be an almost religious experience for my mother. I still didn't see it as anything other than the overwhelming love that a mother (or a grandmother) was *supposed* to feel for her child.

In 1968, we moved to Ithaca, New York, so that my husband could study for his masters degree in art at Cornell University. We hit the Cornell campus the day the black power groups were taking over Willard Strait Hall, the student union building.

And we walked smack into the hippie movement. I merged with the hippie philosophies with the ease that most people merge into traffic. My husband and I became close friends with a group of young black artists, and espoused the cause of oneness and equality for all. I felt . . . truly felt . . . the importance of "making *love*, not war," and I understood the richness of the inner life that I touched when I meditated and "*om*ed." Not that I really knew what I was doing when I meditated.

Instead of knowing that I was reaching union with a God of which everything is a part, I felt that I was touching into my inner self. It felt good, even if I didn't know what this inner self was. But, as I said, I could recognize the richness and depth of what I was doing.

Still as concerned with fashion as I was as a youth, I grew my hair long and straight, wore jeans and Indian prints and paisleys, and utterly disdained anyone over thirty (except my mother who, with her mystical leanings, seemed to fit into the sixties). I loved this period of my life . . . yet I still didn't associate my desire for world peace and freedom and love for all people and respect for our planet with any form of spirituality. It was just *fun*.

I also didn't realize that deep, mystic spirituality could also be fun.

In fact, I'm not sure that I even knew that I had a spiritual side. And I certainly didn't think that I am, in truth, a spiritual being having a human experience. It was all body and mind for me. My body functioned well, danced well, looked good, and remained slender. My mind quickly grasped complicated intellectual concepts and I loved long-into-the-night discussions of the meaning of existence.

Occasionally, late at night, I would have a bizarre experience that I had also had when I was a child. I would awake with the certain knowledge that eternity and infinity were real and were true. Then I would try to get a mental grasp of what eternity meant: How was it possible, intellectually, for there to be anything that *never began* and would *never end*? I could not understand it. My mind was incapable of grasping the concept. Fear would wrack me, and I would break out into a cold sweat. I simply could not solve the meaning of eternity. And since I never thought of the existence of spirit, the entire idea was simply too much for me to bear, so I rejected it utterly. I scorned it. I scorned all ideas of spirituality along with it. How could something exist that I couldn't understand? I was smart; I was capable; if I didn't understand it, it couldn't exist.

I abandoned God.

Fortunately, God didn't abandon me.

As I lived my life . . . worked at a wonderful career as an investment advisor . . . raised my beautiful daughter . . . taught her and learned from her . . . those wonderful twists of fate that could only be caused by some sort of Divine playfulness were not lost on me. I could laugh at the fact that my maiden name was Money and I was working as a stockbroker. I could bless the circuitous events that led me to my wonderful home on a mountain, in the middle of a forest, with three waterfalls in our backyard. I could recognize the presence of some guiding power at work through me when I gave especially good advice . . . or when I had a "feeling" that something good was going to happen . . . when I wrote . . . or when I thought about a client, and s/he would call seconds later.

I didn't recognize the *mysticism* inherent in these experiences, however, for quite a while.

Perhaps the first time I realized that something truly spiritual was happening to me was during a dream I had shortly after my mother's death. She and I were the same age . . . in our mid-thirties . . . and we were sitting in a room that I clearly recognized as the kitchen of my childhood. We were discussing her death.

"I don't think we had any unfinished business," she commented. "I think we loved completely, and I believe we both understood each other, and communicated all the things we needed to say. What do you think?"

In the dream, I remember thinking for a while. Finally, I said, "There is one thing that I wish I had done," I said to her. "I wish I had recorded your voice."

She just smiled. And I awoke.

One week later, my family went to visit my mother-in-law in Florida. Out of the blue, she handed me a cassette tape. "I have no idea where this came from," she said, "but apparently we had the tape recorder going some time when we were all together, and I thought you might want to have the tape. Your mother is talking through most of it."

I was stunned. And grateful. And I *knew* where the tape had come from. For the first time, I really felt the presence of a mystical connection to some higher power.

The first time I truly grasped the oneness of all things, and really understood and felt what my mother had felt as she gloried in the beauty of nature, my husband and I were driving to Sedona, Arizona. We had been on a business trip to Phoenix, and had decided to take a side trip. As we rounded a bend in the road, out of nowhere there arose a panorama of red-orange buttes and mesas, rising up out of the earth in magnificent configurations of magical shapes.

It was breathtaking. Literally. We stopped the car on the side of the road, got out and were bathed in a strong, healing energy. I felt the energy as part of me . . . as me . . . and as the Earth. I felt the energy as a oneness.

And I finally recognized that, like my mother, I am a mystic. I began the long and wonderful journey toward learning how to incorporate this mysticism into my everyday life.

I began to answer for myself the question: How do I *use* the mysticism within me? How can anyone work with the mysticism that is inherent in all of us?

Let's begin now to explore the seven steps that I used to bring this blessing into my everyday life.

STEP ONE:
HONOR YOURSELF

What does it mean to honor yourself?
And what does it have to do with mysticism?

We hear it from everywhere we turn: If we want to have something worthwhile to give to others, we must first take care to cultivate it in ourselves.

We can't give away what we don't have.

If a mystic is a person who honors the sacred in all that is and recognizes that s/he is a part of all that is, it follows that the mystic must first honor himself or herself. Otherwise, there is no honor there to give to others.

We humans are essentially four-part beings: We have a body, a mind, emotions and spirit or soul. To honor ourselves, we must hold sacred all four aspects of our essence.

THE BODY: WHAT WE SEE

Most of us think of ourselves first and foremost as a body. This is the part of us that we see . . . the part of us that seems most real. (It is also the part of us that particle physicists say is not real at all. We are, they say, molecules of matter held together by space, or energy. These molecules are themselves mostly space. When we reduce our bodies to their smallest microscopic atom, it too is energy, and we find that, from this perspective, we are "no thing" . . . nothing but energy. We are made of the same energy that infuses all else that exists.)

That aside, we do nevertheless *appear* to have bodies. Our energy fields are informed by boundaries that make us denser than air, less dense than rocks (usually). And since this energy is localized, bound, into what we know as "us," we have to *care* for these localized energy bundles we call our bodies.

At this point I want to take a rather large digression and talk about what I learned about the sanctity of the body . . . from St. Catherine of Siena.

I have, for the most part, always taken care of my body. I have eaten well, exercised, meditated, done everything (most of the time) in moderation. In my search for sacred mysticism, however, I tended to forget my body. It was something I dressed in wonderful clothes, applied lotions to and looked at in the mirror. It had nothing to do with my newfound mysticism . . . or so I thought.

Until I went to Italy.

Now no one would *ever* picture an Italian mystic sitting cross-legged on a mountaintop. Italian mysticism is replete with voluptuous art, lush landscapes, passionate music, and unbridled joy. It is very much a mysticism of the body.

As our tour group approached Siena, our guide, a storyteller, stand-up comedian and mystical soul named Lorenzo Epifani, told us the story of St. Catherine. A Dominican nun, she became a symbol for women everywhere when she was chosen to rescue the papacy from Avignon and bring it back to Rome, a mission which she successfully completed. When she died, her home church in Siena requested her body as a holy relic. So did the Dominican nuns in Rome. No agreement was reached. So the Dominicans received St. Catherine's body . . . and the church in Siena received her head.

A saint? . . . beheaded by the Church after death? . . . because her physical self was a desired relic? I was appalled by the barbarism. And I said so.

16

"If the Church believes that it is our *souls* that are holy, why is there so much disgusting emphasis on body parts?" I railed at Lorenzo.

He just smiled. "Do you eat?" he asked me.

"What does that have to do with my question?" I countered. "Of course I eat."

"Then you also honor the body," he said with a beatific smile. "Go into the church. Be open-minded," he urged.

"No way," I protested.

In the end, I gave in to Lorenzo's persuasiveness and my respect for his brand of joyful mysticism. I entered the church. It was silent . . . utterly. A priest was saying early mass at the altar. The energy in the church was calm, peaceful, palpable . . . really quite wonderful. I walked to the glass display case holding St. Catherine's perfectly preserved head. And I was filled with the same peaceful silence . . . a stunning stillness . . . that filled the church. I could *touch* the energy in that church.

And I knew that there was a holiness, a sacred presence, there. I also knew that yes, the body is indeed a part of the mystical self.

So how do we honor the sacred in this part of us we call the body?

The first thing we must do is take proper care of our bodies. We need to eat sensibly, exercise, maintain a moderate weight, get enough rest and sleep, surround ourselves with an attitude of joy. We need to avoid substances that are harmful to us. We may need to take nutrient supplements. There are many approaches to these things, and a myriad of excellent books and tapes that tell us how to care for our bodies. I won't outline any specifics here; I'll just say that we need to find an approach that works for us and do it. Our bodies must be healthy if we are to enjoy mystical experiences in our everyday lives. Pain and physical problems will destroy utterly the ongoing joy of mystical experiences in our normal lives. (I recognize that physical illness can lead us to our mystical selves, and I know that unique, one-time, mystic experiences such as the many reported near-death experiences are often caused by pain and suffering. I am talking about achieving these mystic moments, not as infrequent, watershed events, but as a regular part of everyday life.)

So instead of talking about routine ways to take care of the body, I want to discuss more esoteric ways of honoring our bodies.

EXPERIENCING ENERGY

Before we can study the intentional experiencing of energy, we must understand and respect the energy that comprises the bulk (or possibly all) of our own physical selves. We must experience this energy in order to honor it. When we have experienced our own energy field, we can move on to sensing the energies of places we visit and people we meet.

I offer you an exercise that may help you. Begin this exercise by sitting or standing in a comfortable place. Hold your hands in front of you and rub them together until they begin to feel warm. Then slowly move them apart. Cup your hands and move them, very slowly, back together again, as if you were forming a ball of air. At some point, you will begin to feel resistance. This resistance is your energy field. You will probably feel a tingling sensation in your hands as well.

This is what your energy feels like.

Now find an object that you cherish. It can be anything at all . . . but it must be something that you know and love. Hold your left hand over the object. (Intuitives say that we receive energy with our left hand and give it with our right.) What do you feel? Do you feel a certain warmth? Or perhaps something almost electric? Whatever you feel is the energy of the object. Note: This may not work for you immediately. Sometimes, for some people, experiencing the energy in inanimate objects takes a while. Be patient. At some point you *will* be able to feel energy.

Next, go outdoors, to a place in nature where the rocks and earth are real, not manufactured. Sit down in a comfortable position, close your eyes, and imagine a beam of energy connecting you to the earth on which you sit. Slowly breathe in, pulling the earth energy into your body; breathe out, moving your own energy into the earth. When you are relaxed, gently hold your hands, palms down, next to the earth. What you feel in your hands is the energy of the earth.

You may notice that most physical energy feels very similar . . . although some sacred places have stronger energy fields than other places, as do some people. You have probably discovered that this energy is very calming, yet electrifying at the same time.

This is the way the energy of all physical things feels. It serves as proof that, since all energy feels essentially the same, it is most likely a part of one entity. Please don't just take my word for it. Experience it yourself . . . and not just once. Experience this wonderful energy every day, if you can.

As we practice these experiences, we come to realize that, if all energy is essentially identical, then most likely *we* are all one. This is a truth that we can learn, not by listening to gurus or priests, but from the energy of our own bodies. And when we honor this truth, we honor our bodies in a deep and mystical way. Conversely, when we honor our bodies, then we honor this deep truth.

THE MIND: WHAT WE THINK

In order to honor each part of ourselves, we also need to respect our minds. Every cell in the body has its own intelligence . . . its own mind . . . and when we are healthy and whole, these cells act perfectly, as they are supposed to act, independent of our thoughts.

It is the part of our mind where we entertain *thoughts* that can destroy the mystic experience. How many times have we all had thoughts pop unbidden into our minds and shatter our peace?

We can't stop these random thoughts, but we *can* choose what input we give to our minds. When we fill our minds with the numbing idiocy of many television programs . . . or the brutal violence in some movies, TV shows and even newscasts . . . or the judgments rendered by our friends, labeling others as bad simply because they are different . . . we have done exactly what the term says: We have *filled* our minds.

A healthy, mystic mind needs to be clear of these peace-shattering thoughts, at least most of the time. I'm not saying that we should never enjoy popular culture. I *am* saying that we should use it in a mindful way . . . quite literally, a "mind-full" way. If our minds are generally filled with peace, these things will tend not to effect us. If, however, these thoughts tend to constitute the bulk of our day, they most certainly will be harmful. What tends to happen is most likely what we intend to happen. We must intend to have clear and peace-filled minds if we are to have them.

We are creative beings, and our power to create begins with our thoughts. We then express these thoughts in words. The words lead to actions . . . and a new reality has been born.

Do we want to create reality from polluted, toxic thoughts? Not if we are serious about experiencing everyday mysticism.

So what do we do to honor our minds? Change them. Literally. Fill our minds with thoughts of gratitude. Begin to say positive things to and about others . . . and about our-selves. Meditate (more about this in another chapter). If we find a negative thought or angry thought in our minds, we should *change* our mind. Replace the toxic thought with a positive one.

Use affirmations if they are helpful . . . but not to the extent that they become meaningless recitations. (I remember taking a workshop on achieving prosperity several years ago. One of the daily exercises was to repeat the affirmation "I am prosperous" one hundred times each day. I would do this while driving to work, but, by the time I got to number 96 or so, I would get confused, forget how many affirmations I had said, and force myself to go back to number one and start all over again. I finally gave up . . . and achieved prosperity in spite of it all. And fortunately, I had no driving mishaps while doing all this.)

Anyway . . . One of my favorite affirmations that I find *is* helpful to me is loosely borrowed from *A Course in Miracles*: "I choose peace instead of this." Another, from the Bible, is simply, "Peace. Be still."

I have found that gratitude works even better than affirmations for me in clearing the mind of negativity. If we express thankfulness for the good in our lives, soon our minds will be filled with images of this good.

If this sounds impossibly boring, let me point out that we don't need to walk around thinking *only* spiritual thoughts. I, for one, love decidedly non-spiritual things like shopping for shoes, buying clothes, trying out new make-up colors. I enjoy my work. I love to travel. I like to have fun. I have what many people call a sarcastic sense of humor. But what it *does* mean is that we pursue our various avenues of work and play without negativity. We *do* from a place of peace and joy.

THE EMOTIONS: WHAT WE FEEL

We must honor our emotions as well, if we are to find mysticism in our everyday lives. When we are emotionally clear, we can receive a great deal of intuitive messages from our feelings. Something makes us excited? It's probably something we should pursue. Another occurrence makes us anxious? We should be careful. There is probably a reason we feel the way we do. Our emotions often signal messages that our minds overlook.

When are we emotionally clear? We have clarity of feeling when we notice, and pay attention to, our emotions, but don't excessively dwell on them. We muddy our emotions when we concentrate on them. We lose our capacity to experience our mystic selves when we let our emotions consume us.

For example, how spiritual did you feel the last time you were *furious* with your spouse or friend? And did it help when you stormed off and nursed this fury by concentrating on it? The horror of "road rage" is another example of emotions nursed to the point of serious illness.

But we are human; we all feel emotions. What can we do about something so natural? We can strive to replace negative emotions (anger, jealousy, spite, fear) with positive emotions (joy, love, peace). It is nearly impossible to laugh and be angry at the same time.

Try this experiment: The heart, we are told, is the center of our emotions. The next time you begin to feel a toxic emotion, notice the feeling, acknowledge that you have it, then move your attention to the area of your heart. Imagine that you are *breathing* into your heart. Then picture someone, a place, a thing or an event that brings you joy. (I often picture my daughter, or imagine that I am petting the belly of my wonderful, loving old dog.)

When we do this, we usually find that the negative emotion dissipates immediately. And with practice, we can do this exercise in several seconds' time.

Next, in your new state of calm, revisit the original emotion for a moment. Was there something that you were supposed to learn from it? Was it telling you something? If so . . . what?

Be grateful for the feeling . . . then let it go.

SPIRIT OR SOUL: WHAT WE TOO OFTEN IGNORE

The fourth aspect of our being is our spirit, or soul. Some people differentiate between the two, defining spirit as that part of Divine energy that resides within all things. Soul, say some, refers to that deep, inner part of us where our truest desires and creative urges reside. In other words, spirit connects us to God; soul connects us to earthly delight. I don't see much difference, since I believe it is all a part of the same energy, but I will discuss the two separately anyway.

Let's start with soul: . . . that deepest part of us where we feel true joy . . . the part of us that few people may know . . . the part of us that craves music, laughter, beauty, love. It is at this level that we know who we truly are in our earthly incarnation. (Sometimes, in this very inner part of our beings, we feel akin to things that have no precedent in our ordinary lives. For example, there is a part of me that feels as if I have been, or ought to be, a Gypsy dancer in New Orleans. Another part of me desires to have long dark hair and to do psychic readings in Sedona, Arizona. Perhaps, if we believe in reincarnation, these soul urges could be attributed to past lives. Whatever they are, and however inexplicable, they are a part of our soul.)

We must nurture this part of ourselves if we are to reach the experience of everyday mysticism. We need to listen to the music we love . . . take long walks in nature. If possible, we can visit the places we crave to be . . . those places that appear in our dreams. On a practical level, we can beautify our spaces . . . perhaps placing a small fountain in our office and letting the gentle sound of falling water soothe us. We must be gentle with ourselves. It is important to the mystic soul to take some time each day to do at least one thing that we truly want to do.

It is not selfish to care for the soul in this way; on the contrary, it will help us to touch the mystical energy inside us; this energy will help us to do everything better.

We *give* from this part of our being. And remember: We can't give what we don't have.

Spirit is a part of the universal energy that acts *through* us when we are clear and willing. For example, have you ever done something really *big*, then wondered later where on earth you got the strength to do it? Or have you written something, only to be amazed that such ideas could come from you? Or said exactly the right thing, at precisely the right time, to a friend, then marveled at the depth of your own wisdom?

These moments of clarity, moments when we feel connected, are moments when our spirit is acting through us. And these moments are always somewhat mystical. We feel energized . . . whole . . . at one . . . at peace.

So why do we tend to have them so infrequently? In a word, ego. The ego demands that we be *right*, that we be the *best*, that we *win*. And when we are acting from our ego, we have set ourselves up *against* others, rather than in connection to them. After all, we can't be right unless someone else is wrong; we can't win unless someone else loses; we cannot be *us* unless there is an opposing, or at least separate, *them*.

We don't need to eliminate our egos in order to be contemporary mystics. We do need to stop letting ego control us. And we need to recognize when this is happening.

That's not as hard as it might sound. It is taking place every time we think of ourselves as superior to, less than, more correct than, not as smart as . . . in other words, separate from . . . others.

"All right," people have said to me when I expound on this. "This is getting ridiculous! Of course we are separate from others. We have different bodies; we live in different houses; work other jobs. We aren't all one and the same."

On the physical level, that objection is true in some ways. Our energy is localized into a dense bundle we call "my body." And *my* localized energy bundle is different from *yours.* Yet what are the chances that I have breathed in a molecule that was once a part of you? . . . or of almost anyone else who has ever lived on the planet? . . . or every animal, plant, rock? The chances are very good, I would say. And if we are all sharing molecular energy on the physical level, we are *really* one on the level of *pure* energy. We are all a part of the same universal energy plane. We are all what many people would call a part of God. When I was a child in my mother's Catholic church, I often heard the term "Mystical Body of Christ." If I thought about it at all, I assumed it was a euphemism for the church itself. Now I realize that it describes who we truly are: Part of the mystical body of all that is holy . . . part of a sacred oneness.

This thought, and the power it conveys, utterly eclipses the petty concerns of the ego as it tries to convince us of our separateness. And this realization . . . this *knowing* . . . that we are part of a greater oneness, is one of the truest everyday mystical experiences.

STEP TWO:
HONOR OTHERS

Does this mean I have to honor people I don't like?
And what about animals?
And the Earth?

As I begin this chapter, I am doing what is currently called multitasking: I am snowed in at home, simultaneously doing my job as an investment advisor via phone and computer, writing, and cooking homemade soup in a crockpot.

My husband has been sitting for most of the day, staring at an internet explanation of vitamin supplements.

Several years ago, I would have been furious with him. I would have called him lazy, ineffectual. Since I have been following the path of the everyday mystic, however, I no longer feel anything at all about what he is doing, because I have learned an important lesson: Honor others.

As I began walking this path . . . really walking my talk . . . I began to notice some interesting things. If I reached out to help someone else, and if this help was authentic and came from my heart and from the stated need of the other person, invariably something wonderful would happen to me.

I might buy lunch for a man who panhandles near my office . . . and receive a letter from a dear friend in the mail. I would stop at the bottom of the interstate off-ramp to give a dollar to the homeless person begging there . . . and my favorite song would begin to play on the radio.

I also realized that this giving made me feel good . . . warm and joyful inside.

A fellow human had asked; I had responded.

I also noticed that, if I tried to give unwanted help or advice to others, the result would often be an argument, and I would be filled with righteous indignation. How, I would think, could these people refuse my help?

When I began to think about it, the answer was clear: They didn't *want* my help. At least they didn't want what I was offering, because I was not offering what they wanted.

I learned a lesson: We aren't giving help when we give a person something he doesn't want, even if we are certain he needs what we have to offer. If we are going to give, we need to give unconditionally. When we attach our own agendas to our offerings, we are not helping others. And we are certainly not honoring them.

I remember a beautiful story told to me by a friend who is a healer. Greg related that he was approached on the street one day by a dirty and disheveled man.

"Can you give me a dollar, sir?" the man asked. "I need food."

"I don't believe you," Greg responded, "and I will give you the money anyway, in the hope that someday you will remember that you were helped simply because you are a fellow human being, and that you will, in turn, help another person." Greg handed the man his dollar.

"Weren't you afraid the man would buy booze or drugs?" someone asked Greg.

"No," he replied. "That isn't my issue. He asked for money, and I gave him money. I can't judge his use of it."

Greg *honored* the disheveled man.

What are the components of honoring others, and what do they have to do with everyday mysticism?

We honor others when we refuse to judge them. This is a hard one. When we first begin our spiritual path, we are used to judging people on a fairly regular basis: "She is too fat," we think . . . or "He is dead *wrong* to do what he does!". . . or "He can't be honest. He makes too much money." . . . or "She's too pretty. She must be a bitch."

We judge because of our inbred prejudices (pre-judge-ices . . . judging before we know). We judge from lack of understanding. We judge because we fear what is different from us and relate to that which is similar.

We are *taught* to judge. It is a lesson we must unlearn on our mystic path.

Every person on the planet has a special and unique purpose in life. My life path is not the same as yours. I have my own reasons for "multitasking" today. I'm sure my husband has his for studying nutrition information. And you have yours for doing whatever it is that you are doing at this moment.

When I first began my spiritual journey, I found it difficult to stop judging. Finally, I learned how to do it. First, I bless the person I would ordinarily judge. Then I express gratitude for some specific thing that person has done for me.

With my husband it's easy. I'm grateful that he loves me . . . that he fathered our wonderful daughter.

With the driver who cuts me off in traffic, it's not so easy. Yet . . . it works if I am grateful for my safety . . . or for an unexpected lesson in the importance of alert driving. Every person . . . every event . . . offers us some gift for which we can be grateful. And when we are blessing and expressing gratitude, the urge to judge disappears. We are honoring the person we might otherwise have judged.

We also honor others when we respect their life choices.

When my daughter was a freshman in college, I had a strong desire that she graduate in an academic field of study . . .

with honors. (And this was on her first *day* of college.) A formal, liberal arts education is important to me.

After one or two days at the university, she announced that she was going to drop out of her program and take courses that she enjoyed.

"You're *what*?" I responded.

"I don't need all this stuff," she said, matter-of-factly. "When I'm out of school I want to work behind the scenes for a not-for-profit arts organization."

At this point in my life, I had barely placed a tentative toe on the mystic path, so you can imagine my reaction.

But she was determined . . . resolute . . . and, even though I was not yet on my spiritual path, I respected her enough to concede that, even though I didn't agree with her, I would support her choice, and help her in any way I could.

It was my first hard lesson in honoring the life path of another, against my own wishes. And it was a good lesson indeed. My daughter is now the highly successful, very happy, and well-respected Director of Development for a large regional arts council.

And I am a humbler person . . . further along the path of everyday mysticism because of the lesson I learned.

Finally, in order to honor others, we need to give what is asked of us, or be honest as to why we choose not to give. Our natural tendency is to give others, not what they request, but what we think they ought to want. These people who ask us for our help are among our greatest spiritual teachers along our mystic paths. They teach us to give unconditionally.

Last summer I was walking from a deli to my office when a panhandler approached me.

"I need food," he said. "Will you help me?"

Unlike Greg's "teacher," mine had asked for food.

"Sure," I said. "Come with me." I took him back into the deli with me, handed the deli owner $5, and said to the beggar, "Order whatever you want to eat. And bless you."

"God bless you, too. Thank you," he said.

I had given him what he asked for. I had honored him. Had he really wanted money for alcohol? I don't know. He asked for food. I gave him food.

I remember an event from my childhood as if it had happened yesterday. My mother and I were spending a lazy summer afternoon at home, when someone knocked on the door. It was a woman, dressed in very tattered clothing, and her daughter, a girl about my own age.

"We are hungry," the woman told my mother. "And we need clothes. Do you have any food or clothes you could give us?"

I thought it was an outrageous request . . . and a very unwanted intrusion on a pleasant afternoon. Not so my wonderful mystic mother.

She invited the woman and her daughter into our home, and prepared soup and sandwiches for them. Then she collected some of her dresses, and asked me if I would be willing to offer some clothes of my own to the little girl. I relinquished some dresses, shirts and pants that I rarely wore.

The mother and daughter ate their fill, picked up the clothes, thanked us with much emotion and genuine gratitude, and went on their way.

"Why did you do that for them?" I asked my mother after our unexpected guests had gone.

"They needed it," she said simply. "And they asked."

It was later in my life when I related this simple afternoon story to Jesus' statement that "Whatever you do for the least of them, you do for me," . . . and His statement, "Ask and it will be given to you." He was teaching us to live the path of the mystic. And my mother was teaching me. It was a power-ful lesson.

Sometimes we are asked to give something which we believe is wrong, or which we are physically, emotionally or financially unable to give.

We honor the other, in circumstances like this, when we honestly and lovingly state our inability to help. Without advice. Without judgment. Without apology. With kindness.

How does all this honoring of others help us on our path-way to everyday mysticism? Always remember that we receive back from the Universe what we give. When we refuse to judge others, we are not judged. When we respect the life choices of others, we find ourselves respected in turn. And when we give to others what they request, our own wishes somehow come true.

The positive energy we receive from honoring others fills us with the strength, blessings and joy to grow in our own mystic journey.

If that were all it takes to honor others, the life of the everyday mystic would be rather pleasant. It isn't all it takes.

When we study the lives of the great mystics, we find that their honoring of others often superseded their love of com-fort, acceptance . . . sometimes even life. They gave, not only what was requested, and not only without judgment. They gave to others, often, even when that giving violated their own greatest needs and desires.

My favorite Christian mystic is the twelfth/thirteenth century saint, Francis of Assisi. Francis was born in the medieval, mountaintop village of Assisi, in the Italian province of Umbria. His father was a wealthy merchant who sold rich fabrics; his mother was a French noblewoman. Near the village of Assisi was a large leper colony, which Assissians had to pass in order to travel to and from their small city.

Francis was appalled by the existence of the leper colony, and attempted to avoid it at all costs.

If he absolutely had to pass the leper colony, he averted his eyes, covered his nose and held his breath against the wretched stench emanating from the rotting flesh of the lepers. If he gave of his great wealth to the beggars from the colony, his disgust was so great that he asked a friend to place his alms into the lepers' hands.

Francis wanted nothing to do with these people. They repulsed him. They offended his upper-class sensibilities.

One day young Francis was riding his horse in the countryside around Assisi, when he was stunned by the sound of a voice speaking to him. The voice instructed Francis to love and embrace what he had hated and despised, and in this embracing, he would find his true joy. Puzzled, Francis rode on, wondering what the message meant.

And there, on the road directly in front of him, was a leper, begging for alms.

This man most certainly embodied what Francis most despised. With revulsion, but with determined faith, Francis decided to obey the voice he had heard. He dismounted, walked over to the leper, handed him an offering, and kissed the rotting hand of the beggar.

Francis was filled with a joy deeper than any he had ever experienced . . . with a love greater than any he had previously known. He renounced his wealth and possessions, and spent the rest of his life working with the lepers and with those who lived on the fringes of society.

Francis of Assisi is a saint because he knew how to honor others. He is a mystic because he saw the face of God in every person to whom he ministered.

Do we have to relinquish everything we own in order to honor others? Do we, like Francis, need to live among those we fear and loathe?

We don't . . . unless that is our calling. I know that such radical mysticism is not my personal calling. We do, however, need to take some cues from Francis' life. We need to recognize that we cannot ignore those among us who live on the edges of society. We must acknowledge that our society, too, has its own lepers. We cannot forget about the homeless, the diseased, children born with the AIDS virus, the disenfranchised. We must not ignore the people on the Earth who are starving. We don't need to live among these people . . . and yet we must never forget that we *do*, in a very real way, live among them. We must help society's marginal souls in whatever way we are called on to help.

Why? Most importantly, because they need it. But also because, if we are to live the everyday mystic path, *we* need it. We need to see . . . to experience our oneness with all people on the Earth. We need to help them, and know that, as the song from *Les Miserables* states, ". . . to love another person is to see the face of God."

Francis teaches us another lesson about everyday mysticism. He is probably most well-known for his love of animals. He went into the Umbrian forests and fields and preached to the birds, the deer, the trees and the flowers. He honored the presence of God in all existence.

We must do the same. And, no, I don't mean that we all must go out into nature and preach to the animals. I do mean that, when we honor the creatures of the Earth, we achieve a feeling of oneness with the Divine energy that pervades all of existence. And to honor others, we must also honor this energy.

Some of my greatest spiritual lessons have come from four-legged, fur-covered creatures that bark. I think it is no coincidence that God spelled backwards is dog. I experience unconditional love everyday when I come home from work. There are my two wonderful dogs, wagging their tails, wiggling their bodies in unbridled joy at seeing me, sniffing my clothes, giving me kisses. They don't care if I have had a bad workday or a bad hair day. They just love.

And that's what God does.

One day last summer, I was sitting on the dock of our home on the St. Lawrence River, meditating. I had my hands outstretched. I stated silently that I was open to receive. And our collie, Tippy, licked my palm. I started laughing. I was receiving universal love from *Tippy*? And then I realized the truth: Of course I was.

Native Americans attach meaning and honor to each animal. If an eagle soars overhead, it is a sign that Great Spirit is calling to us. A dog symbolizes (and lives) loyalty, and teaches us the lesson of being loyal to our own truths. The bear teaches us introspection, and the dragonfly shows us the way to break through illusion and travel from the spirit world to the physical world.

We need to recognize that, whether we live with animals, or near animals, we must treat the animal kingdom with respect. I'm not going to make a case for vegetarianism, although it is a very pure way to honor animals. Indigenous tribes routinely eat the flesh of animals . . . but they never do it without expressing gratitude to the animal for the gift of its life. They treat animals as sacred.

We must do the same, if we are going to experience mystic oneness with them. Do we need to do this in order to be everyday mystics? Yes, we do. We need to honor all things. Remember . . . what we give, we receive.

St. Francis preached to the flowers as well as the birds. He acknowledged that the Earth itself is part of that vast "otherness" of the Divine, that is really our oneness with all that is.

What? Yes, I do know what I am talking about. We often treat the Earth as if it is something other than ourselves. We pollute it. We trash it. We kill its natural plants in order to put unnatural Astroturf on our lawns. We forget to stop and feel the energy coming from the Earth. We forget that, as the Neville Brothers sing:

> The sacred waters . . . give us life
> The sacred air is our breath
> The sacred Earth, our Mother, she sustains us
>   From our birth until our death
> My heart knows . . . my Spirit grows
>   On this sacred ground.
> Where the turtle lays her eggs is sacred ground;
> Where the eagles make their nest is sacred ground;
> Where the bears lay down to rest is sacred ground;
> Where the wolves raise their young is sacred ground;
> *Wherever any living creature sets its foot is sacred ground.*

If we are to walk the path of the everyday mystic, we must learn to honor all other people. We must respect our animal companions. We must honor and care for the Earth itself.

We must learn that, when we look at anything that exists, we are looking from the eyes of God, into the eyes of God . . . no matter what we see.

STEP THREE:
BE BEFORE YOU DO

~

. . . Or what you do will not be a reflection
of your deepest truth . . .

Think of the deep implications of the last suggestion in
the previous chapter. If we are looking at all things from the
eyes of God, into the eyes of God . . . then what does that
make us? At our deepest level, who are we . . . really?

If we are to *be* before we *do*, who and what is it that we are
to be?

We who have taken seminars dealing with spiritual truths
have often heard the expression, "We are spiritual beings having a human experience." But what does this really mean? As
spiritual beings, who are we?

Take a minute to become silent, and to ponder these ques-
tions. Close your eyes. Concentrate on your breathing. Become
calm. As you breathe in the stillness, you may realize that there
is a part of you with whom you are connecting . . . a sacred part
of you that has nothing to do with the body you have. Imagine
this part of you going back to your childhood. Is this part of
you the same now as it was when you were a child? . . . Can
you feel the experiences of your childhood . . . your youth . . .
your young adulthood? Can you remember them? Was there a
part of you then that is still a part of you now?

This eternal part of you . . . the *you* that was there as a
child and is here now. . . is not your body. The cells in our

bodies renew themselves on a regular basis, and the body we have now is not the same body we had even one year ago.

What is it, then, that is the same about us? It is that part of us that Deepak Chopra calls the "observer," that many spiritual teachers name the "Higher Self"; it is that part of us that doesn't age . . . that doesn't change . . . that doesn't die. It is the part of us that we call spirit, or soul.

Feel the presence of this part of you. This is *who you really are*. This is who you must *be* before you can truly *do* what is your highest good in this life. As you complete your meditation, bring this part of you back to your everyday life. Acknowledge it in all that you do, for this is the part of you from which you must act, if you are to have the life of an everyday mystic.

This part of you is part of a Divine Oneness with all things . . . a part of God, if you will.

We knew who we were when we were born. Why did we forget?

Life taught us to distrust, and eventually to disregard and abandon our knowledge of our inner spirit. Life often did this through well-meaning parents, who had themselves forgotten their true identity.

Did your parents, or another authority figure, ever say to you in consternation, "Just who do you think you are?"

From the point of view of the everyday mystic, we could now answer, "I am a manifestation of Divine Oneness . . . a part of the Universal God."

A seven-year-old who has just broken his mother's best vase is not going to find this answer on the tip of his tongue. So he believes he is wrong. He forgets the strength and eternalness of his spirit. He feels flawed . . . not deserving. He begins to classify his actions as "good," or "bad." And he begins to act from this state of perceived inferiority.

As long as we are acting from this perspective, we are acting from a perceived separateness from others. We perceive ourselves as different than . . . better than . . . worse than . . . *other* than others. And we compete. We fight for the riches of the world in an attempt to be better than others . . . in an attempt to regain a sense of worth that we knew we had in the past. Somewhere along the way, we lost it, we believe. We didn't, of course. We just lost *sight* of it.

We need to claim our true selves again.

In my business, I advise people and help them achieve their personal goals through financial planning. When I first ask clients about their goals and dreams, the comment I most often hear (or some variety of this comment) is, "Well, I want to *have* a lot of money, so I can *do* what I want to do. Then I will *be* happy."

No. They won't. But I work with these wonderful people to help them invest properly so that they will be able to meet their financial goals. This I can do. But I can't make them *be* something which they aren't. So, along the road of our relationship, I try to praise my clients. I tell them how valuable they are to me as people while I discuss their path to their net worth. And I hope that I help them personally as well as materially, because unless they know how to *be* what they most deeply desire, having all the money in the world won't help them achieve this state of being.

Sometimes it's funny. One of my coworkers came into my office several weeks ago.

"What are you so happy about?" he asked.

"I'm happy about the fact that I'm happy," I answered.

"No," he reiterated. "What are you happy *about?*"

I just smiled. "I'm happy because I'm happy," I responded.

"You're nuts," he said, throwing up his hands and walking out of my office.

I laughed, and returned to my work. I know that this state of *being* what we desire is the state from which we must *do* whatever it is that we do on this path of everyday mysticism. Otherwise, what we do will truly not be a reflection of who we are at our deepest level. We will not be acting from that part of us that is one with God.

So how do we achieve this beingness?

The short answer is, "We don't." We don't *achieve* a state of being, because achieving involves doing. Confusing? Yes . . . but it's a very important distinction. Everything that it is possible for us to be, we already are. (There are some things that are impossible for each of us. I will never be a football star. I will never be a father.) Nevertheless, there are certain states that it is possible for all of us to live within. We all have the right, and the ability, to be joyful . . . to love . . . to feel peace . . . to feel a oneness with all things. And, as I said, we already are all these things. Everything that exists in the Universe is available for us to use. We don't have to *have* anything or *do* anything to *be*.

And we don't have to search in distant places to find these things we want to be. We don't have to travel to discover who we are. Our essence, and our entire beingness, is where we are, all the time, wherever we are, whatever we are or are not doing. It is within us. It is in exactly the place where we forget to look.

There is an old story about a group of wise men who are attempting to hide the secret to happiness from humankind.

"Let's hide it on top of the highest mountain," one sage suggested.

"No," another commented. "Someone will find it there. Let's hide it at the bottom of the sea."

"That won't work either," added another man. "How about in the branches of a tree?"

That idea, too, was rejected. There was no place where humans wouldn't look for the secret to happiness . . . no mountain too high . . . no ocean too deep . . . no forest too dense.

Suddenly one of the men had an idea. "I know where we can hide this treasure. It's a place where people *never* think to look. Let's hide it *within each person*. They'll never look there."

And that is where the secret of happiness is hidden. Inside each of us. It's also the place where everything we are is found.

To connect with this deep part of who we are, and to find our true being within, we first need to be in contact with our inner self on a regular basis. We need silence. We need to meditate. We need to listen. I will talk more about these practices in later chapters.

Once we have gone deep within, and found our true essence, we need to listen carefully to our desires. We need to pay attention to the things that excite us. Do we want happiness? . . . Love? . . . Do we want to create art? . . . Or create a family? These inner desires are reflections of who we are as individualized parts of Divine energy. They define who we are.

Okay. Imagine that we have meditated, listened to the desires of our innermost self, and we know that what we want more than anything else in the world is to be joyful. And the furnace has just broken down, the dog has run away, our spouse is yelling at us, it's 2 A.M. and our son isn't home from the party yet, we have a report due at 8 A.M. and we haven't started it.

What do we do? We don't. We *be*. And, in order to be anything, the first thing we have to master is an old trick borrowed from the business world: Act as if.

There is joy within us. We know this. To be flooded with this joy is our deepest desire. So we *act as if* the joy, which is unquestionably a part of us, is present to us at this moment. How? We express gratitude for the joy in our lives. We thank God, in whatever form we envision God. We bless our lives.

Suddenly, as if by a miracle, we begin to touch into some of the things that bring out this inner joy. We are thankful that we have a job. We are grateful for our son and our spouse.

And, when we can feel this joy as a part of our being, we give it away. Whatever we want more of, we must give away. What is the best way to get a hug? Give a hug. What is the best way to receive a smile? Give one.

So, in the middle of the chaos that is our life, we begin to feel the presence of joy . . . and we turn to the spouse who is yelling at us and tell him that we are grateful for his love. (Yes . . . he will think we're crazy, but do we really care? He will also begin to feel joy. And as he feels it, he will, automatically give some back to us.)

We have to *be* before we *do*.

Or . . . what we *do* will not be a reflection of who we are at our deepest level. Let's look at our chaotic scenario from another perspective. Suppose, rather than acting from the truth of who we are inside, we forget this truth, and begin to yell back at our spouse. And we get angrier and angrier with our son. Will this help us achieve the happiness we desire? You bet it won't. And it won't help our attitude toward our work or our life. It may even give us a headache. Or worse.

If we are acting from the truth of who we really are, however, the results may not be dramatically different at first, but we will certainly feel better. And whatever we do will be done from this place of truth. Over time, because we tend to manifest in the outer world what we are in our deepest self, our results will be startlingly different.

We each have our own inner desires . . . our own dreams and deepest qualities. Some will desire peace more than joy. Others will find that creating is their greatest inner quest.

As individuals, we must honor these different inner blessings. We all, however, have one thing about our essence that

STEP THREE: BE BEFORE YOUR DO

we share with all other people, places and things. As the
Indian mystic Sri Auribindo states:

> The master of existence lurks in us
> And plays at hide and seek with his own Force;
> In nature's instrument loiters secret God.

This is more than a beautiful poem. It is a deep, deep truth
of who we are. We are all beings with the secret God "loiter-
ing" inside us. When we have learned to act from our inner
qualities, we must then learn to act from our inner God. If we
do this, we will be most perfectly walking the path of the
everyday mystic.

When I began my mystical journey, I meditated often,
asking the question, "What must I do to serve?"

The answers I received were not what I wanted to hear at
first. (I think I wanted to be told to move to a red-rock butte
in Sedona, Arizona, wear Gypsy clothing and do psychic
readings.)

The messages I received were nothing like that. "Give only
love," I heard, over and over. And "Be a blessing."

At first it didn't sound nearly as exciting as being a psychic
in Sedona. But as I began to take the instructions seriously, I
realized that it made no difference to the planet, to me, or to
anyone I might encounter, if I wore funky clothes and lived on
a mountaintop. When I gave love to others, however, it made
all the difference in the world . . . to them . . . and to me. And
when I attempted to "be a blessing," I received a wealth of
blessings in return.

The underbrush was cleared from my mystical path.

When I gave love, I was giving that part of myself that was
my most true essence . . . that was a part of God.

The Christian mystic John of the Cross said, "My occupation: Love. It is the only thing I do."

I'm not there yet, but I have reached a point where I understand what he is talking about. I am approaching that occupation.

In my opinion, my favorite Christian mystic, Francis of Assisi, shows us an almost perfect way to *be* before we *do* in his beautiful prayer:

> Lord, make me an instrument of your peace.
> Where there is hatred, let me sow love.
> Where there is injury, pardon,
> Where there is doubt, faith,
> Where there is despair, hope,
> Where there is darkness, light,
> And where there is sadness, joy . . .

Francis is praying to act from the truth of his inner being, his inner, lurking God. I would like to look at this beautiful poem line by line.

"Lord, make me an instrument of your peace." Francis is not praying for the ability to *do* anything. Rather, he is asking that God act through him . . . use him as an instrument of peace. Francis is not asking to be the player or the resulting music. He is asking to be the instrument through whom God plays and peace results. This is the epitome of *being* before *doing*. We, too, as we walk the path of the everyday mystic, can be instruments of peace. Each day, when we wake up, and before we go to bed, we can center in our hearts, breathe peace within ourselves, then bring this peace with us as we go through the day. By being peaceful in our own hearts and minds, we breathe peace out to others we meet along the way.

"Where there is hatred, let me sow love." We have children killing children in our schools. We have become so angry and hate-filled that we have even coined a name for this anger:

road rage. But what can we do? We are each only one person living in this angry world.

We can refuse to honor this hate. We can sow love instead. The next time someone cuts us off in traffic, instead of cursing him, we can send him a blessing. When we are met with an angry frown, we can give back a smile. We can recognize our oneness with all things, and project love out onto all the people in the world. We can pray.

It sounds simple, this acting from what we are. And the beauty of it is that it *is* simple. As the commercial says, "Just do it."

"Where there is injury, pardon." Forgiveness is one of the most powerful tools we have for changing, not only ourselves, but the world as well. When someone hurts us, we often hold anger and resentment toward this person. *We* hold it. When we forgive, we release this negativity from ourselves, and from the world. When our heart is forgiving, there is one less injured heart in the world.

"Where there is doubt, faith." How often do we stop ourselves from doing what we know is the kind thing . . . just because we don't see how it would do any good? We fear that we might be ridiculed. We are afraid that we aren't right. We doubt. Usually, our first intuitive impulse to do something for someone else is the correct impulse. We need only to have faith that it is. And act on this faith. We will be acting from the truth of our being.

"Where there is despair, hope." We are stunned by the masses of humanity suffering on this planet. Everywhere we look, we see news of people starving. We hear of wars . . . of natural disasters. We can't change these things. But we certainly *can* refuse to add to the despair felt by so many about so much. We can inject words of hope into conversations about world suffering. We can donate to people who need help and to organizations that help these people. Again, we can pray.

"Where there is darkness, light." One of the things we are at our deepest and most essential level is a being of light. When we choose to shine this light . . . through kindness, love, warmth . . . onto others, we are, in a very real way, bringing light into the darkness.

"And where there is sadness, joy." There is enough sadness in the world. We have already talked about the fact that, when we give something to another, it grows . . . it expands . . . it comes back to us a hundredfold. The gift of even a small amount of joy in the world can ease the sadness immeasurably.

When we have reached the point in our journey where we are living with the inner truth that we *are* love . . . we *are* joy . . . we *are* light, we will be living with the greater truth that we are a part of God.

And we will be well along the path of the everyday mystic.

STEP FOUR:
HONOR YOUR
COINCIDENCES

Does that mean I have to pay attention
to books that fall off the shelf?

And to song lyrics?

The first fact that we need to acknowledge in honoring our coincidences is that there aren't any.

My friend Annie quotes an old adage when she says that "coincidences are God's way of remaining anonymous."

Deepak Chopra calls coincidences "conspiracies of improbabilities," and urges us to pay very careful attention to the guidance they offer.

Neale Donald Walsch, in *Conversations with God: An Uncommon Dialogue, Book 1*, implies that coincidences are ways in which God communicates with us, and quotes God as saying:

> Ask me anything. Anything. And I will contrive to bring you the answer. The whole Universe will I use to do this. So be on the lookout . . . Listen. The words to the next song you hear. The information in the next article you read. The story line of the next movie you watch. The chance utterance of the next person you meet. Or the whisper of the next river, the next ocean, the next breeze that caresses your ear—all these devices are Mine; all these avenues are open to Me. I will speak to you if you will listen. I will come to you if you will invite Me. I will show you then that I have always been there.
>
> *All* ways.

Once we begin walking the path of the everyday mystic, we *must* listen; we must honor our coincidences . . . we must follow where they lead us. As mystics, we acknowledge that we are a part of everything that is, and because we are all part of the same vast energy field which we call God, the extraordinary can become ordinary for us. The mundane can lead to miracles. The fluttering of butterfly wings can indeed change the course of history.

Since I have begun this journey into mysticism, I have not only learned to honor coincidences; I have come to rely on them.

For example, six years ago, my husband was working as a realtor, and wanted to get the listing to sell a home in a beautiful lakeside community about twenty miles from Syracuse, New York, where we lived.

He asked me, our daughter Laura, and Ken, her husband, to go with him to see this home.

"Pretend you're buyers," he said. "If the owners think I'm bringing buyers, I might get the listing."

Up for a Monday evening adventure, we piled into his Jeep.

The house was awful.

As we were leaving, I suggested that we have dinner in a quaint village restaurant.

It was closed.

As we walked down the pretty main street of the town toward another restaurant, we passed the office of another real estate agency. In the window was a picture of a gorgeous Greek Revival home in the country, with 183 acres of land.

"Why don't you get the spec sheet on that house," I suggested to my husband. "We can look at it after dinner." We were not in the market for a house, but it sounded like fun.

He and Ken went into the real estate office. Laura and I secured a table for four at our second-choice restaurant.

Soon my husband, Joseph, and Ken arrived, listing in hand.

"Here it is!" Joseph said happily, handing the sheet to me.

It described a *totally* different house. In a *tiny* village boasting somewhere around three people, and perhaps a hundred cows . . . a good ten miles further out in the country.

"This is the wrong place!" I exclaimed. "I don't want to see *this* place."

"Come on," Ken urged. "We can see a country sunset."

Reluctantly, I agreed.

We drove down gorgeous, curving country roads, lined with cornfields, wildflower meadows, farmland, and old evergreen forests.

Following the directions on the spec sheet, we arrived at an unpaved road leading up a mountain. There was one driveway, amid a forest of trees and wildflowers. We turned into the driveway and came upon what appeared to be . . . a two-car garage . . . still under construction.

"I'm not even going to get out of the car. This is nothing but a *garage*," I said with indignation.

Joseph was not so fussy. He opened the door to the Jeep . . . and I heard the sound of water.

"What's that?" I asked, getting out to explore. I walked around what turned out to be a large house, not a garage, and there, not forty feet from a beautiful deck at the foot of a hill, was a twenty-foot waterfall, nestled among granite boulders and forest. A stream flowed by the deck.

My childhood summers were spent near Laurel Falls in the Great Smoky Mountains. These falls looked the same. The smell of damp earth was the same. The energy was the same.

Joseph walked over to me.

"I'm home," I said.

"You haven't even looked at the house," he reminded me.

"It makes no difference," I answered. "I'm home."

The inside of the house turned out to be beautiful, in fact. On the drive home, however, doubt set in. It was a *very* long drive to and from my place of work.

The next morning, my boss walked into my office.

"You're one of two people here getting a portable computer system," he said. "That way you can work from home when you choose to. Would you like to try it?"

We bought the home.

Oh . . . and the name of the forested mountain that has not one, but *three*, waterfalls, now in my backyard? . . . Mystic Mountain!

Yes . . . I *rely* on coincidences!

I want to digress for a moment here and answer a question that you may not be asking. No, these coincidences . . . these magical moments . . . are *not* the sum and substance of mysticism. Mysticism is a deep and profound life path; it is a recognizing and an experiencing of ourselves as one with God. It is the feeling of this oneness as a deep and passionate love. But these wonderful little "Post-it notes from the Universe" can lead us to a deeper sense of the mystical . . . of how all of life works together. And they can be a very powerful *result* of practicing everyday mysticism as well.

These little miracles, disguised as coincidences, are God's way of nudging us in the direction that is right for us. They are reminders . . . proof that, as we co-create our reality, there is a Divine co-creator who works through us.

Still, coincidences are important . . . and they can be fun as well.

I have mentioned that I work in the brokerage industry. One day I was wondering, in meditation, if this career was the appropriate one for me. Suddenly, I was struck with two facts: In numerology, my life-path is an Eight. This stands for abundance, management, and prosperity. If numerology has any merit at all, this indicates that I should spend my life, in some way, working with the manifestation and management of abundance. That offered me some direction. Then I realized, probably rather slowly, the most obvious indicator that my career was not only appropriate, but perfect for me: My maiden name is Money. Really.

We must honor our coincidences . . . even as we have fun with them.

In *The Celestine Prophecy*, James Redfield states that "The First Insight is an awareness of the mysterious occurrences that change one's life, the feeling that some other process is operating."

That other process is God. The mysterious occurrences are what we choose to call coincidences. And they make a profound impact on our lives . . . if we allow them to.

My husband and I were driving home from a visit to our dear friends in New Jersey one Sunday afternoon. We needed to be home by 5:30 in order to pick up our dogs at the kennel where we had boarded them. We were running late, and getting hungry.

We were passing the exit for Roscoe, New York, on Interstate 17, and we both love the Roscoe Diner.

"Let's stop and get something quick to go," I suggested.

My husband eagerly agreed.

We parked the car and entered the restaurant. Out of nowhere, I heard what Neale Donald Walsch calls "a voiceless voice."

"Eat in the restaurant," it said.

Now I've been on the path of the everyday mystic long enough to know that I should at least consider messages like this.

"I have a feeling that we should eat here," I said to my husband.

He has been aware of my path long enough to trust my instincts.

"OK," he agreed, "but we won't be able to get the dogs until tomorrow."

"Eat here," the voiceless voice said.

We sat down and enjoyed a meal.

We finished eating, got into our car and turned onto Route 17. Not two miles away, we saw red lights flashing on both sides of the highway. Shattered glass was everywhere. Several ambulances roared down the highway, their sirens wailing. Police officers were beginning to cover several crushed automobiles with tarps. The accident had happened about thirty minutes before.

It had taken us thirty minutes to eat.

I said a large prayer of gratitude, and an even larger prayer of blessing for those who weren't so lucky.

Yes, these occurrences can change our lives in ways that are indeed profound.

A major part of honoring our coincidences is being aware of exactly *what* they are and *how* they operate in our consciousness and in our lives.

I've heard friends who are beginning to place a tentative toe on the mystic path say gleefully, "There are no coincidences in life. God will provide for me all that I need."

Satisfied and comfortable, they plop down on the couch, pick up the remote, click on the TV, and wait for God to take care of them . . . and they wait . . . and they wait some more. And finally they decide that the mystic path doesn't work.

It *does* work. And God . . . or Allah . . . or Great Spirit . . . or Yahweh . . . or the Universe . . . or Wakan Tanka . . . or whatever we choose to call divine energy . . . will indeed provide. But providing won't come on a silver platter or in Tiffany boxes (usually).

Let's go back to our friend on the couch, and assume that he is desperate for a way to consolidate debt. He flips on CNBC and the first thing he sees is a commercial for a company that gives home equity loans. Is this a divine "coincidence?" You bet it is!

Will it solve his problems? No. But, if he *recognizes* the coincidence as perhaps having merit, and if he gets up off the couch and calls the toll-free number, it just *might* ease his dilemma.

Coincidences require trust, cooperation, and *work* on our part. We have to pay attention. We must be willing to act on our "hunches." We need to trust the Universe and follow the leads given to us through coincidence.

And yes . . . at times this feels like leaping off a cliff into a dark and unknown void. Other times it is such fun that we berate ourselves for not doing it sooner. However it feels, divine guidance . . . for that is what coincidences are . . . requires our cooperation. As the old saying goes, "God can only do *for* us what He can do *through* us."

It is at this step on the path to everyday mysticism that many people begin to falter. It requires work. It requires trust. It requires acceptance and embracing of ideas that seem foreign.

It is relatively easy to honor ourselves (or to fool ourselves into believing that we do). Honoring others requires little outer work, and we can pretend to honor others without true interior honor. To *be* before we *do* seems rather peaceful at times . . . and again, if we want to *pretend* to be at one with the Universe, it is relatively easy to do so. (This, of course, doesn't make us everyday mystics. It makes us charlatans. But you know what they say, "You can fool some of the people some of the time . . .")

Whether or not we're being honest with the first three steps, it's rather pleasant to think of ourselves as everyday mystics . . . people who see and honor the sacred in all things.

In honoring coincidences, on the other hand, we can't fool ourselves. We have to listen and *hear* the messages we receive

. . . then have the courage to act on them or to *choose* to reject them.

We can't ignore them.

A major problem that everyone on the path of the everyday mystic will face is this: Which of our "hunches" are divine coincidences? Which ones are irrational mutterings? Which songs on the radio are giving us guidance? Which are only making noise? Which chance meetings are significant, and which are merely chance?

Distinguishing the false from the true may be the hardest part of honoring our coincidences. Over the years, I have learned through trial and error how I tell true "coincidental" guidance from meaningless messages and random thoughts. This method works for me; another method may work better for you.

First of all, when intuitive thoughts come into my head, for *me*, they seem to come from the *back* of my head. (This is very unusual. Most people receive messages from a different part of the head . . . but all I can rely on is what works for me.) Alternately, they come as a *knowing*, rather than a wondering. When they don't come from my head, they arise in my solar plexus.

And they involve *no emotion at all*.

I learned this by experimenting with things that were completely insignificant to me. If I attempted to test intuitive hunches about things which meant a great deal to me, I lost my objectivity, and received no meaningful messages.

One experiment that was helpful to me involves elevators. You might want to try it. Stand in front of a bank of elevators, and ask yourself which one will reach your floor first. Take your *first* thought. Keep doing this. Notice whether or not your first thought is accurate. If it is, on a fairly consistent basis, notice where it appears to come from. Notice how you feel. And take this warning: If you experiment with events that are important to you, you *will* vest the outcome with emotion, and your investigation won't work.

Then try the experiment with another stimulus. Test again where your information comes from. Whenever you receive an intuition from that part of yourself which appears to offer accurate information, act on it. See what happens.

This process may take a while. Everyday mystics aren't developed overnight. Be patient.

When we receive a thought which immediately brings about fear or apprehension, it is most likely *not* guidance through coincidence. To receive messages from the Universe, we need to be "in the flow" of the Universe. The divine energy of the Universe is, wholly and entirely, *love*. And, as *A Course in Miracles* states, fear is the opposite of love. Where there is fear, love cannot enter. Neither can coincidental guidance. (I am speaking here of guidance along the path of *everyday* mysticism. Under emergency circumstances, such as times when we are in harm's way, guidance can indeed come instantly, even if we are afraid.)

And what of chance happenings? How do we distinguish the meaningful from the superficial? On a certain level, I believe *all* things that happen to us and around us are meaningful. They don't bring us coincidental guidance, however, if we don't notice them. And I believe that we tend to notice those events, grand or trivial, which will have special meaning for us. We notice those things which lead us along our paths.

These chance happenings may give us information which is superficial or crucial.

One of my acquaintances relayed to me the story of how, everywhere she went, she heard women discussing breast cancer. She turned on the radio and heard public service announcements about the disease. She decided to have a mammogram . . . and, yes, cancer was discovered . . . early enough that she is now entirely cancer-free and in remission.

That was indeed a crucial message. I remember one which I received that was *very* superficial, yet certainly acted as proof that coincidences do guide us.

I had found a beautiful set of hand-painted dishes in a Sundance catalog, and I felt that they would be perfect everyday tableware for our new home. I was driving home from work, thinking about whether or not I should order them. Ahead of me, a traffic light turned red. As I stopped at the light, I noticed the license plate on the car ahead of me. It said "SUNDANCE." I ordered the dishes.

Deepak Chopra lectures that we can know when we are receiving guidance from the Universe when we encounter what he calls a "conspiracy of improbabilities." We have this situation when events happen together that are unlikely to occur together regularly. My experience with the SUNDANCE license plate is an example of this.

Another "conspiracy of improbabilities" that happens to me involves books. When I am looking for information, somehow the book containing that information is given to me. My friend Magdalena insisted that I borrow her vintage book of mystic poetry written by Sri Auribindo. She literally thrust it on me. I had known nothing of Auribindo's work, yet it has become a major influence to me on my own mystical path.

As I was writing this book, I had an urge to go shopping for clothes (not an unusual urge for me). I asked my husband to go with me, and at the last minute, felt that I *had* to go to a bookstore instead. I *thought* I wanted coffee from the store's café, but, as I was walking toward the café, a book seemed to glow. I walked over to it. It was the story of Francis of Assisi . . . my favorite Christian mystic. It contained quotes that I needed for my writing.

Honor your coincidences. They are God's way of honoring you.

STEP FIVE:
SEEK THE SILENCE

Uh-oh . . . Now I'm going to be told that I have to meditate to be a mystic!

We live in a world that is filled with noise . . . with distractions . . . with chaos. This external world, wonderful though it can be, is nonetheless the enemy of everyday mysticism.

Unless we learn how to *use* the cacophony to tune into our inner mystical selves, the world can quite literally destroy our inner peace.

It has taken me a long time to achieve this priceless ability. As I write this chapter, both the Dow Jones Industrial Average and the NASDAQ have plummeted by more points than ever before in the history of the exchanges. It is a sunny Saturday in April, and, even though I don't quite know what to do on Monday, today I feel a perfect peace. Within, I am calm . . . in harmony.

Yesterday, as I was working at home, listening to a CNBC broadcast of the big crash, I realized that, in spite of what was going on around me, I was serene then as well. There was a part of me . . . a deep inner stillness . . . that was completely untouched by the events of the outer world. That deep silence is always with me.

It wasn't always that way. During the crash of 1987, the chaos within me matched, or exceeded, the turmoil in the markets. I was shocked . . . numbed . . . frightened. I was beside myself.

And that is, quite literally, what we are when we don't know how to access the silence. We are *beside ourselves*. Not at one with ourselves. Not in tune with ourselves. Not at peace. We are not with ourselves at all. We are somewhere else. *Beside ourselves.*

Think about this concept for a moment. How often have you been, for instance, walking along a beautiful path through a forest . . . or driving past rolling hills . . . or in the presence of a loved one . . . *and your mind is miles away, having an argument with someone who has wronged you?* You are not with yourself. (In fact, depending on the extent of your mental wanderings, you may be so far away that you aren't even close enough to be *beside* yourself.) Your body may be walking in peace, but your mind is roiling in tumult. And at times like this, you can't even be remotely conscious of your spirit.

Being able to be in a very real way *with* yourself is central to the experience of everyday mysticism. In order to feel at one with all that is, we must first feel at one with our inner selves.

So how do we achieve this? We seek the silence.

There are several aspects to this practice (and it is very much something which we must *practice* . . . daily). In order to recognize, and touch into, the silence within us, we first need to be comfortable with external silence. We need first to spend time daily in silence. We need to practice meditation. We need to learn how to access our inner stillness, no matter what is going on around us. And, perhaps most importantly, we need to pray.

The first thing we need to do is carve out a time . . . a sacred alone time . . . *every day* . . . when we can be absolutely still inside. We need to be without the stimulus of other people, of a television set, or a book. (No, having your morning coffee while watching CNN doesn't count.)

OK . . . I can *hear* the protests. We all have schedules that leave little time for breathing, let alone silent communing with ourselves. We don't have the time, we moan.

Yes, we do. Each one of us, if we really think about it, can find some time during our busy days to be alone and silent. Perhaps we need to wake up a half-hour earlier, or go to bed a bit later than usual. Maybe we can take a walk during our lunch hours. Some of us can close our office doors, shut off our computers and phones, and be still.

If we live near untouched nature, being in the outdoors brings us quite naturally closer to the silence.

I began to realize the need for silence years ago, when I would feel anger for no apparent reason. It would rise up inside me, fill my abdomen and chest cavities, and settle in the region of my throat. To release it, I would find some logical reason to yell at my husband. This didn't help at all. I knew I needed a better solution.

I started to wake up an hour earlier each morning, and take walks in nature. I would watch the sunrise . . . say good morning to the crow sitting in the topmost branches of the tree at the end of our driveway. In spring and summer, I picked wildflowers that were growing alongside the road. In winter, I marveled at the beauty of an early-morning sun turning the ice on tree branches into webs of sparkling crystal. In autumn, I looked in awe at the glorious, multicolored painting created by nature.

I still do this.

When I first began my walks, however, I found that my mind went wild with random thoughts. As I looked at the beauty of the earth around me, my mind wanted to rush back to yesterday's market close, and leap forward to dwell on potential difficulties of the new day. This was disconcerting. After all, I was trying to find silence . . . and my mind was making noise.

This is natural. This will always happen. The mind is acting as an "attorney" for the ego, which is saying, "Me . . . me . . . pay attention to me." The more I fought this intrusion into my peace, the worse it was. My fighting itself was mental noise.

Finally I learned to breathe in the energy of the day, and breathe out my random thoughts. First, I expressed deep gratitude for the day . . . for the stillness . . . and for the workings of my mind. (The mind and the ego like to be acknowledged.) Then, I imagined that the earth energy surrounding me was a glowing white light. I breathed this light into my body, and released my cares and worries (which I pictured as gray clouds.) It took a while for me to be able to do this effectively, but, after years of practice, I can say that it works wonderfully well for me. And now, I can do it in seconds.

Wayne Dyer describes another way to quiet the mind. He suggests that we picture our minds as deep pools. On top of the pool are dead leaves . . . floating debris . . . ripples in the current. These are our random and unwelcome thoughts. Just below this pond scum, if you will, the waters are still in motion from wind . . . rain . . . sinking objects. At this level of mind, we have fewer thoughts. As we allow our minds to sink deep within the pool, however, we reach a place of primal silence. We find a depth that is untouched. This is the place where our minds find true silence.

As you begin to work out your own methods of accessing silence in your world, do not use this silence as a time to work through your problems, or to formulate new ideas. *Use the silence as silence.* When you are able to find communion with the stillness each day, you will naturally find new answers to life situations . . . but they won't come during your periods of silence. They will come unbidden . . . as coincidences . . . as insights . . . as messages from other people.

Before these insights begin to come regularly, however, you must have periods of silent communion. (Think of this word, communion. It means, quite literally, "with oneness.") That is exactly where the silence takes us. To that inner place where we are with oneness . . . with all that is.

Being in the silence is not the same thing as silent meditation, but meditation is very much a part of the silence we need in our daily lives if we are to grasp the joys of everyday mysticism.

There are many wonderful books and tapes describing meditation techniques, and classes offered in meditation practices, so I am not going to describe *how* to meditate. Instead, I will talk about the importance of *doing* it, and the results that daily meditation can bring to us as we walk the path of the everyday mystic.

When we are simply being in silence, we are achieving deep stillness. Meditation is more than this. It offers us the ability to touch into the stillness *and* the "still, small voice" within us. When we enter meditation, we ideally go into a state of absolutely silent, yet totally alert, awareness. We are within that part of ourselves that some people call our "Higher Self." We are with our spirit . . . with that part of ourselves which is eternal . . . with that part of ourselves which is also a part of everything else that is . . . and which is a part of God.

If being in the silence brings inner peace, meditation brings clarity and a deep and profound knowing.

In silence, we quiet our thoughts. In meditation, we go to a place where thoughts do not exist . . . and from this place of no-thought, we receive all knowledge.

Deepak Chopra describes this place as "the gap." It is, he explains, a place of "pure potentiality." In this "gap" between thoughts, we are at one with the consciousness of the Universe; we are in touch with the consciousness of God. We have the potential to know all that the Universe knows. We have the potential for Divine guidance.

The experience of deep, meditative awareness is one of the truest forms of mysticism. This silent stillness, at times, can be deeply passionate. We can feel profound love . . . absolute peace. We can receive insights that will change our lives.

Or not.

And it is this "or not" that more often than not stops people cold in their practice of meditation. We hope, each time we sit to meditate, that we will receive intuitive visions. We expect to be given profound insights. And sometimes we just get gas. Or we fall asleep. Or, as happened to me last month, we remember that the next day is a friend's birthday.

So why do we need to meditate, if we don't always receive guidance? *Because sometimes we do.* And when we do, that guidance is more profound than anything else we have ever been given. Because sometimes this guidance comes, not *during* meditation, but because we have trained our minds *through* meditation. Without the ability to experience silent awareness, we would miss the messages. Without meditation, we will be unsure of the state of awareness when we experience it.

I use several different meditation techniques. I sometimes simply follow my breathing. Other times I use a guided meditation. At times I use music. Sometimes I let the sound of the waterfall bring me to deep awareness.

Find a means of meditation that works for you. Practice it. Relax into it. Be gentle with yourself if you don't instantly achieve "Nirvana." Keep practicing. Meditation *will* change your life.

One of the major ways in which meditation and silence can change our lives is that these practices increase our ability to touch into silent awareness at any time . . . for just a moment, or for a much longer period of time . . . whenever we choose to do so. Once we know how to reach a state of stillness, we can go there no matter what is happening around us.

I have described the feelings of peace I experienced during the recent market crash. But we don't need cataclysms in order to choose to access stillness within.

Last winter, I was driving into the city to meet my daughter for a workshop we were attending together. Snow was falling hard, the wind was creating drifts by the side of the road, and I was caught in bumper-to-bumper traffic . . . travelling at somewhere under two miles per hour. The entire world appeared to be a white wonderland. It was absolutely gorgeous.

My car phone rang. It was Laura.

"Mom," she said. "Are you all right? Are the roads OK?"

"I'm wonderful," I answered. "The snow is beautiful, I have strong coffee in my thermos, and I'm listening to music. It's a pleasure to see all this pristine beauty surrounding me."

She was silent for a moment.

"You're in the middle of a snowstorm . . . and you're *wonderful?*" She asked. Then she laughed. "Only you, Mom. Only you could be joyful in a blizzard. I'll see you at the conference. Drive safely."

I felt this peace and joy because I had taken a few minutes to go into the stillness within. I had drawn that stillness out, and it had given me peace. Laura was wrong about one thing, though. It isn't only me. We can all be joyful in any type of blizzard, weather or otherwise, if we can access our inner silence.

Like meditation, there are many ways to do this. I prefer to move my breathing to the area of my heart, and to imagine that I am breathing white light into my body. Then I imagine this light filling my entire body, and extending out around me. The presence of this white light represents God to me. And it brings me peace. Instantly.

So does gratitude. All I need to do is say, "Thank you for the beauty that is surrounding me," and really *mean* it . . . truly *feel* grateful . . . and I am bathed with peace and joy.

Probably the most important, and least understood, aspect of seeking the silence is the practice of silence as prayer.

Many of us grew up with the idea of prayer as a beseeching and begging for help from an external, maybe fatherly, possible judgmental, perhaps even vengeful, God. Western cultures depict this God as a bearded old man, somewhere up in the sky, who answers our prayers (or doesn't), then condemns us to a place called hell, or elevates us to a place called heaven. We go to Him when we have problems, and we beg for His assistance.

He (for remote Gods of most cultures are men) is above us, both physically in His sky home, and metaphysically in our perceptions of ourselves as lesser beings. He is greater than we are . . . and He never deigns to communicate with us, except through our religious leaders.

An old joke goes something like this: When we talk to God, it's called prayer; when God talks to us, it's called schizophrenia.

From the point of view of the mystic, that couldn't be further from the truth. The mystic holds that it is madness *not* to realize that God talks to us. Always. We just don't listen.

It is in the silence that we begin to realize that our entire lives are prayers. Consider this beautiful poem/song from *Gitanjali* by Indian mystic Rabindranath Tagore:

> When my play was with thee I never questioned who
> Thou wert. I knew nor shyness nor fear, my life
> Was boisterous.

In the early morning thou wouldst call me from my
    Sleep like my own comrade and lead me running
    From glade to glade.

Of those days I never cared to know the meaning of
    Songs thou sangest to me. Only my voice took
    Up the tunes, and my heart danced in their
    Cadence.

Now, when the playtime is over, what is this sudden sight
    That is come upon me? The world with eyes bent
    Upon thy feet stands in awe with all its silent stars.

This poem, which describes the very heart of a child's experience of God . . . that joyful feeling that all of life is a wonder . . . the idea that we awake, live and *play* with the energy of grace all the time, also describes perfectly the experience of the everyday mystic at prayer.

This "sudden sight" that comes to us as we grow is given to us by the churches, which tell us of a God whom we must awe as we stand at His feet. Play with God? Never. That would be a sacrilege. We must worship.

Of course, we must. But the definitions that religions give to worship usually make us *separate* from God. To experience God once again as we did as a child, we must remove this separation. We must learn to experience a God within us and within all that is . . . a God with whom we cannot only love, but also play and live every moment of our lives.

This living with God is true prayer.

I'm not going to tell anyone how to pray properly, for there are many ways to do this, and with prayer, there is really no such thing as "proper" or "improper." Prayer, to me as an everyday mystic, however, involves being aware of the sacred in all things. It involves feeling gratitude for the experiences of life. It is a sense of being "in the flow" of divine energy.

When we are in this flow, we are indeed talking to God. And God is talking to us. We need silence to learn how to do this initially, so that we can be truly *with* this energy at all times.

And God will indeed talk to us . . . in millions of ways.

One evening, for instance, I was driving to my new home in the country. It was almost 10 P.M., dark, and the roads at that time were new to me. Cornfields lined the curving roads.

"I must be nuts to be out here all alone in the middle of cornfields in the dark," I muttered to myself.

I felt a warmth envelop me, and I heard a "voiceless voice" say, "You are never alone."

We are not alone. Ever. When we truly *know* this and *trust* it, we are in the most pure form of prayer.

And we are well along our path to everyday mysticism.

STEP SIX:
HONOR YOUR
"DARK NIGHTS"

Do I have to have a "dark night of the soul"
to be a mystic? . . .

Isn't there an easier way?

As I write this, it is Good Friday . . . a singularly appropriate day on which to write about the "dark night of the
soul," as this period of spiritual agony was called by Christian
mystic John of the Cross.

Very few people have nights as dark as did Jesus. Three
years into his ministry, at the young age of 33, his teachings of
love and forgiveness gaining widespread acceptance, he was
nonetheless betrayed by one of his own disciples. His friends,
when asked to be with him as he acknowledged this betrayal
and its fatal punishment, denied him or fell into sleep. When
he begged that the cup of his destiny be taken from him, he
ultimately resolved that, "Not my will, but thine, be done."

Nailed to the cross, Jesus cried out, "My God, why hast
thou forsaken me?" Then, in a moment of insight and light,
He surrendered to what He knew was His divine mission.
"Into thy hands, I commend my spirit," he cried out.

The story of Jesus' last days is a devastatingly accurate
description of a classic "dark night of the soul."

Jesus experienced the agony of betrayal . . . of loss . . . of
fear . . . and the pain of aloneness . . . followed by a total surrender to a will greater than his own: the will of God. This

SEVEN STEPS TO EVERYDAY MYSTICISM

happened to him, in the course of two days, not once, but twice.

This dark night of Jesus teaches us many things. During our lives, we have *many* dark nights. The mystic path is not a road with one very large bump, followed by smooth, straight byways. The mystic path is filled with bumps. Over and over again we encounter obstacles; over and over again, we surrender to the truth of these obstacles, and work our way through them.

But Jesus' story, like the story of every mystic, doesn't end with the surrender of his spirit on the cross. Three days later, after being entombed, he rose again . . . into the eternal life that is available to us all on the mystic path.

We learn, from Jesus . . . from the teachings of other mystics . . . and from our own "dark nights" . . . that, at the end of the darkness, there is indeed light. This light is greater than any light we have ever previously known. This light is the recognition of our oneness with God . . . our own personal resurrections.

We are not, as we walk the mystic path, comparable to Jesus as evolved sacred beings. But we are walking the same road.

And always, in all parts of life, it is the occasional darkness that helps us to realize, and grow in, the light. If we did not each night fall into sleep, we would not last long in the daylight. If we did not see shadows, we might not acknowledge the light which creates the shadow. Without the "dark night of the soul," we would not complete our mystic path; we would be camped out at some comfortable spot alongside this path.

If we are to live the life of the everyday mystic, then, we *must* experience "dark nights of the soul."

What exactly is this phenomenon? Very few of *us* can expect physical crucifixion during our lifetimes. How do we know when we are in a dark night, and how do we get out of one? And what do they involve?

In order to begin to answer this question, I'm going to go off on a digression that may not, at first, make much sense. But bear with me. Since its inception, the stock market has followed an upward path most of the time. The value of quality equity investments continues to grow greater and larger over time. This journey toward higher ground, however, is not a straight path upward. Ever so often we meet with a "bear market." The prices of stocks plummet; the wealth of the market goes into a free-fall; investors experience fear, panic, despondency, terror. All that we thought we had, we question. How do we survive these horrendous crashes? We go through them. We look for opportunities. We look for guidance. And eventually . . . when we least expect it . . . the market begins once again to rise.

The "dark night" could be described as a "bear market of the soul."

Unusual though it is to compare the mystic path to the stock market, it is nonetheless a very good analogy. When we encounter a "dark night of the soul," we feel as if we are in a free-fall. Nothing seems to go right for us. We feel terror . . . we don't know where to turn. We try to turn to God, but our fear or our anger or our doubt blocks out all light. We feel lost. And we must go through this. We must look for signs of guidance along the way. And, like a financial bear market, this bear market of the soul will end. For Jesus it ended in resurrection. For us, at least, it will end in light.

We have "dark nights" when our plans and dreams are in complete conflict with God's goals for us. Painful though they may be, these periods of darkness prepare the way for us to proceed on a path that is correct for us. They prepare us for our true life work as everyday mystics.

Sometimes these "dark nights" are dramatic and virtually instantaneous. If actor Christopher Reeve had not fallen from a horse into paralysis, would he have become such an eloquent and powerful spokesperson for the handicapped? I don't know. But surely there is some sort of divine irony in "Superman" being paralyzed. And certainly the accident must have been a "dark night" for Reeve.

Other times, along the mystic path, we meet many obstacles . . . events that wear away at us . . . that beat us down . . . that come close to breaking our spirit. And through these painful times, we learn our strengths. We learn to trust the energy of the divine . . . the only place we have left to trust, in some cases. The Biblical story of Job is an example of this type of tortuous "dark night."

My dear friend Jane has had such a life. The daughter of an outcast mother in the South, she was raised by dear family friends. Her first marriage was to a brutally abusive alcoholic. This marriage produced two beautiful daughters. One of Jane's daughters died of cancer. The other spent time in prison. Jane's godmother contracted and died from cancer. On Jane walked on her path. She walked *through* these trials . . . and emerged into the light where today she lives as a great spiritual educator and minister and teacher. These traumas took many years to resolve themselves. They were a dark *decade* of the soul.

My mother's early path as well was one of constant erosion of the spirit. The child of an abusive father who, in one of his drunken outrages, flung her into an open fireplace and broke her brother's legs, she was orphaned at four years old. She was placed into a series of equally abusive foster homes, culminating in the episode I described earlier in the book. She met her first "dark night" early in her life.

Christian mystic Francis of Assisi, in 1224, two years before his death, climbed the rugged Umbrian hillside of Mt.

Alverna, where he entered a forty-day period of prayer, fasting and solitude. "My Lord Jesus Christ," he cried out. "I pray you to grant me two graces before I die: the first is that during my life I may feel in my soul and in my body, as much as possible, that pain which You, dear Jesus, sustained in the hour of Your most bitter passion. The second is that I may feel in my heart, as much as possible, that excessive love with which You, O Son of God, were inflamed in willingly enduring such suffering for us sinners."

Shortly after uttering this prayer, Francis received the stigmata, which he bore for the rest of his life. And on his deathbed, racked with illness, he nonetheless sang with joy the "Canticle of the Creatures," his beautiful poem in praise of God in all of nature's forms.

When I began to study the mystic path I was walking, I wondered about the purpose of the "dark night of the soul." I began to question the truth of its existence, at least in the lives of ordinary people having mystic experiences. And I feared that I was not truly on a mystic path, because I did not seem to have had the great tragedies in my life that plagued the likes of Jesus, Francis of Assisi, Christopher Reeves, my friend Jane or my mother. My friends who are Vedic astrologers studied my astrological chart and said, over and over, "You have a life that is blessed."

For this, I am deeply grateful. Yet the question remained a nagging one. In all my readings about mysticism, the "dark night" was stressed. Could a person fortunate enough to have a blessed life be a true mystic?

I was living in the midst, not only of a very good life, but also within a deep and heartfelt closeness to God. I *knew*, deep within myself, that I was one with the energy of the divine, and that everything else I encountered was also a part of this divine spirit. I felt the presence of light within, and almost daily, I felt washed with a joy as cleansing as a spring rainfall.

I knew no dark nights. I contemplated, but rejected, the possibility that being angry with my husband, or encountering a market crash qualified as a "dark night of the soul."

My life was, and is, thankfully, blessed.

Then one night I was in a midst of a deep meditation, feeling a profound and passionate union with the infinite and the eternal. Into my mind leaped the unbidden and unwanted thought, "What if none of this is true? What if it all ends at death?"

I felt sheer terror . . . panic . . . dread. I felt as if I had suddenly awakened from a beautiful dream into a reality where I had lost my anchor. I didn't know where I was, how I had gotten there, or how I was supposed to return to my wonderful world of joy and union.

For the next several months, I sleepwalked through my life, which appeared on the surface unchanged. But oh, how empty I felt inside. I had lost my connection. I performed my daily activities robot-like, feeling as if my light had been unplugged . . . extinguished.

I kept up my silent morning walks. I meditated, although my meditations seemed like hollow caves of illusion. I continued to pray. I looked to my coincidences for guidance. I kept walking, even though the path seemed, not so much covered with brambles and thorns, but covered with . . . nothingness.

Then one morning, I awoke . . . and the emptiness was gone, as suddenly as it came.

And I realized that I had indeed experienced a "dark night of the soul." I further realized that there are two very different, and equally valid, types of "dark night." There is the Situational Dark Night, in which our entire lives collapse, our world is overturned and our solace . . . our very foundation . . . is shattered.

And there is the Spiritual Dark Night, in which our lives may proceed quite normally, yet our souls feel abandoned . . . empty . . . dead.

I realized that they are equally powerful, because both types of "dark nights" lead us to the same thing: a greater realization of our mystic oneness with God and with all that exists. These "dark nights" shake up our lives in one way or the other. They make us pay attention. They make us *aware* of the truth of our existence: that we are spiritual beings, and that we must nourish our spirits even in the midst of chaos or emptiness. We come to know, in a deeper way than before, that, if "How do I get out of this fear?" is the question, "God" is the answer.

And these "dark nights" take us into the light . . . and, perhaps more clearly than ever before, we *see* the light. We, who so recently have been disconnected from the light, are grateful for its return. We are en-light-ened. We can *live* in the light. We are walking daily, and with deep awareness, on the path of the everyday mystic.

We are walking with God.

STEP SEVEN:
HONOR GOD

Which, like the circle of life, takes us back to the beginning, where we start the process over at a higher level, since we are all a part of God . . .

What is God? Or, as some might prefer to ask, *who* is God? Before we can *honor* God, we first need to know what we are honoring.

Since the beginning of time, human beings have recognized the existence of some sort (or sorts) of Supreme Being.

The Unity tradition teaches the following: "God is all, both visible and invisible . . . This One that is all is perfect life, perfect love and perfect substance."

In the Hindu tradition, this being is called "That," and, as Deepak Chopra says, "I am That. You are That. All this is That. And That is all there is."

Mystical Judaism refers to this being as "Yahweh," or "I *Am*."

Native Americans speak of "Great Spirit."

Jesus referred to God as "Our Father."

Walter Starcke, in the book *It's All God*, says that "God is Omnipresence. God is Omnipotence. God is Omniscience itself. The words become plural, infinite, all-inclusive, and impersonal."

In *Conversations with God: An Uncommon Dialogue, Book 1*, God says to Neale Donald Walsch, "Those who believe that God is All That Is *and* All That Is Not, are those whose understanding is correct."

But, after all the definitions that could exist in the world are said and done, we are still left with the overriding question, "*What is God?*" It is easier to discuss what God is *not*, with the understanding that God is *everything*, and with the further understanding that some acts and definitions do not accurately manifest this Divine Everything-ness.

Many religions claim that they alone have access to the one God. All others . . . all who are not part of their group . . . are condemned to an eternity in hell. This kind of judgmental exclusiveness has nothing to do with God.

Nor do arbitrary rules. Several years ago, St. Patrick's Day fell on a Friday during Lent, and the bishop of the Syracuse diocese declared a dispensation so that diocesan Catholics could eat corned beef with their cabbage. In nearby Rochester, the Bishop declined to grant a dispensation, so Catholics in Rochester traveled to Syracuse to eat meat. Forbidding the use of a certain food . . . or believing that what one does at home is wrong, but it is perfectly acceptable in the next city . . . is not only superstitious nonsense, but it also has absolutely nothing to do with God. (Here I am not condemning those who choose to abstain from something they enjoy as a spiritual practice. These personal choices can be very fulfilling. But rigid rules regarding trivialities are ridiculous . . . at least in my opinion.)

The reality of God also has nothing to do with how we view God . . . although these views can certainly affect how we choose to honor God. Western religious traditions have tended to personalize their ideas of God . . . to picture God in the image and likeness of our physical form. Eastern spirituality has experienced the idea of God as an energy force, superior to the physical form. Indigenous persons find God personified in the sun . . . the moon . . . the earth . . . the sky.

In the end, perhaps all definitions of God are accurate if they serve those who define. In the end . . . and always . . . we are alone . . . and all one . . . with our concepts of God. We must, in this alone-all-oneness, come to know God on our own. This knowing of God is the most important aspect of the mystical path.

To me, God is an energy that infuses all things . . . God is Love . . . God is Peace. God is in all things and *is* all things. And if God is all things, then no-thing . . . nothing . . . is not God.

But in your path of everyday mysticism, you most certainly do not have to agree with my concept of God. You do need to find your own God-presence in your life, however. And when you find that which is God for you, you must honor this presence.

How do we do this?

All spiritual traditions have their own ways of honoring God. Some honor God as a person. Others honor God as an energy. Still others look at God as a divine and passionate lover. Let us look at some different traditions of honoring God.

Native American spirituality is deeply bound to the Earth, and to all the creatures on the Earth. Native Americans honor Grandfather Sun, Grandmother Moon, Father Sky, Mother Earth . . . and every creation which walks, swims, flies, grows to the sun, sits upon the Earth, or is kissed by the wind and the rains.

Hopi chief Thomas Banyacya, quoted in *Wisdom Keepers*, says that:

> The supreme law of the land is the Great Spirit's, not Man's Law . . . Let us live in peace and harmony to keep the land and all life in balance. Only prayer and meditation can do that.

Leon Shenandoah, a chief of the Onondaga Nation, quoted in the same book, states:

> I myself have no power . . . Real power comes
> only from the Creator. It's in His hands. But if you're
> asking about strength, not Power, then I can say that
> the greatest strength is gentleness.

Are these ideas of living in peace and harmony . . . of keeping all life in balance . . . of the strength of gentleness . . . of prayer and meditation . . . honoring God? Most definitely they are.

Jewish scholar Daniel C. Matt, in his book *The Essential Kabbalah*, states his belief that,

> If God's gaze were withdrawn for even a moment,
> all existence would be nullified. This is the secret
> meaning of the verse: "You enliven everything." So
> divinity flows and inheres in each thing that exists.
> This is the secret meaning of the verse: "God's pres-
> ence fills the entire world." Contemplating this, you
> are humbled, your thoughts are purified.

This humbling before the pervasive existence of God is also very much honoring God.

Many Eastern traditions express a passionate honoring of God, rather than the peaceful intellectualism found in Native and Jewish teachings.

From Islam, we have the gorgeous words of Sufi poet and mystic Jalaluddin Rumi, who writes:

> It is said, Lend unto God,
> So give a loan of the leafage of the body,
> That a garden may grow in your heart.

Give a loan, diminish the body's food,
So you may see what the eye has never seen.
When the body becomes empty
God fills it with musk and luminous pearls.

How very different is this diminishing of the body's food from an abstinence from corned beef on St. Patrick's Day! And how much more a personal honoring of God!

One of the most famous, and most well-known, Hindu mystic poets of the twentieth century, is Rabindranath Tagore, who wrote, in "Canticle 103" from *Gitanjali*:

In one salutation to thee, my God, let all my senses spread
    Out and touch this world at thy feet.
Like a rain-cloud of July hung low with its burden of unshed
    Showers let all my mind bend down at thy door
    In one salutation to thee.
Let all my songs gather together their diverse strains
    Into a single current and flow to a sea of silence in one
    Salutation to thee.
Like a flock of homesick cranes flying night and day
    Back to their mountain nests let all my life take its voyage
    To its eternal home in one salutation to thee.

If this is not honoring Tagore's God, then there is no such thing as honor.

Taoist mystic Lao Tse defines God in his ancient collection of wisdom, the *Tao Te Ching*:

Look, it cannot be seen—it is beyond form.
Listen, it cannot be heard—it is beyond sound.
Grasp, it cannot be held—it is intangible.
These three are indefinable;
Therefore they are joined in one.

From above it is not bright;
From below it is not dark:
An unbroken thread beyond description.
It returns to nothingness.
The form of the formless,
The image of the imageless,
It is called indefinable and beyond imagination.

Stand before it and there is no beginning.
Follow it and there is no end.
Stay with the ancient Tao,
Move with the present.

Knowing the ancient beginning is the essence of Tao.

The sense of awe and wonder expressed by Lao Tse is indeed an honoring of God.

Christian mystic Francis of Assisi, in his *Praises of God*, calls out to God:

You are love,
> You are wisdom.
> You are humility,
> You are endurance.
> You are rest,
> You are peace.
> You are joy and gladness.
> You are justice and moderation.
> You are all our riches,
> And you suffice for us.
You are beauty.
> You are gentleness.
> You are our protector,
> You are our guardian and defender.
> You are our courage.
> You are our haven and our hope.

You are our faith.
Our great consolation.
You are our eternal life,
Great and wonderful Lord,
God almighty,
Merciful Savior.

It is said that Francis, enraptured by God in all things, would run into the Umbrian fields, and call out to flocks of birds that their every song should be a song of praise to God. It is further reported that, after Francis exhorted them, the birdsong was far more beautiful than before. Francis' honoring of God was the entirety of his life. In his book of rules, he writes:

> Nothing, then, must keep us back, nothing separate us from him, nothing come between us and him. At all times and seasons, in every country and place, every day and all day, we must have a true and humble faith, and keep him in our hearts where we must love, honor, adore, serve, praise and bless, glorify and acclaim, magnify and thank, the most high supreme and eternal God, Three and One, Father, Son and Holy Spirit, Creator of all and Savior of those who believe in him, who hope in him, and who love him; without beginning and without end, he is unchangeable, invisible, indescribable and ineffable, incomprehensible, unfathomable, blessed and worthy of all praise.

In this beautiful text, Francis literally "says it all" about honoring God. If the everyday mystic honors God in this way, he or she will walk always in light and love and God.

But we are not Francis of Assisi, nor are we Rumi or Tagore. We are citizens of the twenty-first century . . . people who must combine our honoring of God with our work, our families, our play and our personal trials. The beautiful truth about the path of the everyday mystic is that these profound masters of mysticism, like us, honored God while doing their work, helping their families, experiencing their very personal joys and pains. In their lives, they were very much like we are in ours. They were not so different from us after all.

And what we need to do to honor God is not so very different from what they did. If we can go through each moment conscious of the love of God in our hearts and in our lives, we will experience in each moment the magic and the mystery of honoring God on our mystic paths. In fact, if we can feel God in our hearts for even *one* moment each day, we will be walking the path of the everyday mystic.

If we can see God in all things . . . if we can find love and joy at the core of our beings . . . if we can truly *know* the silence that is the "peace that passes all understanding" . . . if we can find goodness and God-ness in everyone we meet . . . if we can let the energy of God act through us, as us . . . we will not only be honoring God, we will be, in our own right, true mystics.

SOME FINAL THOUGHTS

Taking a look backward in history . . .
And a look ahead to your mystic path

The path of the everyday mystic is indeed wonderful, filled with blessings and joys . . . but, in contemporary society, it is not always an easy path. Actually, it never was.

In order to understand some of the difficulties we may face as everyday mystics, I want to use this "last look" to go back into history and explore a bit about the tradition of mysticism, particularly in the Christian Church.

For millennia, a spiritual dichotomy has existed . . . and this dichotomy was made even more pronounced after the life of Jesus Christ. This duality is, at simplest levels, a difference in the ways in which we observe reality.

Some of the followers of Jesus viewed him objectively . . . as *the* Son of God . . . as the *only* begotten Son of God. Jesus was God. This meant, clearly and objectively, that he *alone* is God. This meant also that we are very much *not God*. Some of the statements of Jesus, if taken literally, support this objective view. "I and my Father are one," he said. And "I am the way, the truth, and the life."

Fundamentalist Christian religions today espouse this objective view of God. They believe, as we discussed in an earlier chapter, in a God who is *out there somewhere* . . . in a place called *heaven* . . . wherever that is. They believe that He is made in the image and likeness of man (although they don't quite express it this way), and they believe that only Jesus is his son. Further, they believe that only through the words of Jesus, as recorded in the Bible (and only certain versions of the

Bible) will we be saved. This God is an objective God who does what WE do. He judges. He meets out punishments. He gives rewards to those who believe.

The roots of Fundamentalism existed at the time of Christ. In fact, the gospels of Matthew, Mark and Luke bear witness to Jesus as a man who was also the Son of God. They chronicle the objective life of Jesus.

At the same time, however, there was another movement among the followers of Christ. It was called the Gnostic movement. The word "gnosis" means "knowing," and the Gnostics believed that, as Jesus knew God, they too could know God . . . through prayer . . . through inner wisdom . . . through internal experience.

The objectivists, for lack of a better word, *believed* in the Divine.

The Gnostics *experienced* the Divine. They *knew* the Divine.

There is a huge chasm of difference between knowing and believing.

The gospel of John, and the apocryphal gospel of Thomas, speak to this knowing. In Thomas, Saying 75, for example, is the following quote: "Jesus said, 'I am the light that is over all things. I am all: all came forth from me, and all attained to me. Split a piece of wood, and I am there. Pick up a stone, and you will find me there.'"

This speaks to a deep knowing that God, through Jesus, and through all things, is indeed *in* all things.

For a while, objective Christianity and Gnosticism lived side by side. As the official Church grew, however, and desired more political power over its people, it became clear that the only way to have this power was to declare that the objective view of Jesus, as explained by the Church, was the correct view.

It is impossible to exert power over one who knows and communicates with an internal God. Gnosticism was condemned as heresy. After this condemnation, there were few acknowledged mystics. Those who were mystics were enfold-ed within the Church. They went into monasteries, convents, or . . . in other traditions . . . ashrams or temples. The rest of the world plodded along, fearful of an external, vengeful God.

In the monasteries and the other places of holy study, these remaining mystics were hardly *everyday* mystics. They had specific places to go to pray and meditate. They had silence and strong, evolved spiritual advisors. They never needed to worry about concerns of the outer world.

They had one job only: to experience their oneness with God.

This dichotomy existed in the world for many centuries. The world moved slowly. Little changed. In the twentieth century, however, change began to accelerate. It reached critical mass in the 1960s. Vatican II opened the windows of the Catholic Church, letting in fresh air . . . for a while, at least. The Dalai Lama was exiled from Tibet, bringing his spiritual mysticism into the world at large. Hippies . . . grubby though they may have looked . . . explored Eastern and Western mysticism. In large groups they learned meditation . . . studied with gurus . . . "*om*ed."

Mysticism, as medical intuitive/spiritual teacher Dr. Carolyn Myss describes it, has gone mainstream. More and more people, especially those who are members of New Thought churches, are seeking mystical union with God. As we walk the path of the everyday mystic, we look around and see that we are not alone.

We see proof of this everywhere we look: the *New York Times* bestseller list *always* has at least one spiritual book highlighted. Oprah Winfrey broadcasts spirituality to her huge viewing audience through her guests and ideas.

In large numbers, we have meditated . . . we have prayed . . . we have experienced, if only briefly, our oneness with the Divine. We have taken the steps to everyday mysticism, and delighted in the path to which they lead.

And then reality strikes. We . . . the contemporary mystics . . . don't have monasteries where we can shut ourselves off from the world at large. We must be everyday mystics *in* the work world.

We must . . . in a very real way . . . be *in* the world, but not *of* the world. Even if we have diligently practiced all the steps to everyday mysticism, we will still reach a point where we will throw up our hands in despair and cry out "How?" . . . "How am I supposed to *do it all?*"

First, there is the problem of time. How, for example, can a single parent of three young children find time to breathe, much less meditate? When we have trouble finding our car keys because we are in such a hurry, how can we make time to find God?

Then there is the problem of self-esteem. Being a success in the world requires a strong sense of self . . . a confidence . . . a strength. Being an everyday mystic requires a *surrender* of self to the Divine.

Being in the workplace demands that we deal with angry customers . . . sell used cars . . . type letters . . . answer telephones . . . program computers . . . select investments . . . fight traffic jams.

Being an everyday mystic speaks of silent communion with God.

How do we deal with our contemporary dichotomy?

We must realize . . . and recognize . . . that it is *all* a part of the Divine: the meditation and the mediation . . . the diapers and the divine insights. Every task we do is a part of Divine Order when we do it with love.

And yes . . . in the work world and in our family lives, we need self-esteem. We are taught (correctly) that we create our own reality. Yet the mystic tradition espouses the letting go of self and the surrender to the oneness of God's reality. Isn't this a contradiction?

Yes . . . and no.

We *do* create our own reality. And when we are living on the path of everyday mysticism . . . when we are creating from our inner oneness with the Divine . . . we are surrendering our *ego* self. And if we are working from our higher inner self, we are also letting go of the outcome of our creativity. We are surrendering it to God to take care of the details.

It sounds easy.

It isn't.

The everyday mystic in contemporary society has to work toward oneness with the Divine while changing diapers . . . standing in unemployment lines or grocery lines . . . or being president of the United States. Sometimes it feels as if we are going crazy . . . as if the chaos of the world is pulling us in fifty different directions (at least) . . . as if the entire *world* is going crazy.

It feels as if we are very much *in* the world *and of* the world. And, in a sense, we are because, at the truest level, *it is all God.*

To live as a mystic in this world, however, we have to realize that, while it is all God, there is a part of all of it that is transitory and changing . . . and a part of all of it that is transcendent and unchanging. We, as spiritual beings having a human experience, won't *always* have to type letters or sell cars. Our physical lives will evolve.

We won't always *be* spiritual beings having a human experience.

We will die.

That part of us that is transcendent . . . our spirit or soul . . . the "observer" . . . the unchanging part of us that is one with the whole of Divine energy . . . will *not* die. And it will not change. This is the part of us that is not *of* the world. It is eternal.

It is this part of us that we need to touch into daily . . . and to *act* from . . . in order to survive as an everyday mystic in today's world.

Here we meet face to face the original Christian dichotomy (no matter what our faith): the objective versus the subjective . . . believing versus experiencing. Both types of faith are, in a sense, correct. It is our job, as everyday mystics, to weave them together.

A part of life *is* objective . . . a part of us, yet not a part of us. I am one with you, but I am not you. And Jesus was indeed the Son of God. As was Buddha. And so are we.

And sometimes when we pray we appear to be supplicating an external God. Other times, in the midst of our silence, we are communicating with the Divine within us.

And sometimes, we're just doing our work, without a thought of God.

Sometimes, it's enough to drive us crazy . . . or drive us to a monastery.

But always . . . in all ways . . . if we are doing whatever we are doing with a loving heart . . . if we are bringing our sense of inner peace and love into the chaos of the world . . . if we are doing our objective work while holding on to our interior mysticism . . . we are uniting these two disparate elements.

We are bridging the dichotomy.

We are . . . one person at a time . . . changing the world.

We are living as everyday mystics.

It will be a wonderful path that you will walk. The path of the everyday mystic will bring you joy that is indescribable. It will bring you "peace that passes all understanding." It will bring you face to face with God in all that you see. It will bring you roadblocks and "dark nights of the soul."

And ultimately, it will bring you home. Have a wonderful mystic journey. Namaste.

BIBLIOGRAPHY

Sri Auribindo. *Savitri, Part One.* Pondicherry, India: Sri
    Auribindo Ashram, 1950.
Chopra, Deepak. *Ageless Body, Timeless Mind.* New York, NY:
    Harmony Books, 1993.
Feng, Gia-Fu and English, Jane. *Lao Tsu's Tao Te Ching.* New
    York, NY: Vintage Books, 1997.
Foundation for Inner Peace, *A Course in Miracles.* Mill Valley,
    CA: Foundation for Inner Peace, 1992.
Matt, Daniel C. *The Essential Kabbalah: The Heart of Jewish
    Mysticism.* Edison, NJ: Castle Books, 1995.
Mizzi, Father Maximilian, OFM. *The Message of Saint Francis.*
    New York, NY: Penguin Putnam, 1998.
Meyer, Marvin, Trans., *The Gospel of Thomas.* San Francisco,
    CA: Harper San Francisco, 1992.
Neville, Charles and Kristin. "Sacred Ground," *All My
    Relations, Mitakuye Oyasin Oyasin.* New Orleans, LA:
    Neville Music (BMI), 1996.
Redfield, James. *The Celestine Prophecy.* New York, NY:
    Warner Books, 1997.
Starcke, Walter. *It's All God.* Boerne, TX: Guadalupe Press,
    1998.
Tagore, Rabindranath. *Gitanjali.* Boston, MA: International
    Pocket Library, 1992.

Wall, Steve and Arden, Harvey. *Wisdomkeepers.* Hillsboro, OR: Beyond Words Publishing, 1990.

Walsch, Neale Donald. *Conversations with God: An Uncommon Dialogue, Book 1.* New York, NY: Putnam's Sons, 1996.